Under the Shadow

Under the Shadow

Letters of Love and War
1911-1917

The Poignant Testimony and Story
of
Captain Hugh Wallace Mann
7th & 5th Battalions
The Queen's Own Cameron Highlanders
and
Jessie Reid

Bríd Hetherington

Cualann Press

Published by Cualann Press, 6 Corpach Drive, Dunfermline KY12 7XG, Scotland.

ISBN 0 9535036 0 7

First Edition 1999

British Library Cataloguing in Publication Data. A catalogue record of this book is available at the British Library.

Printed by Panda Print, Dunfermline.

Under the Shadow is dedicated to:

Catrìona, Iain, Feargus and Finlay;

the memory of their great-grandparents and great-great-aunts Jessie, Winnie and Dine;

the memory of Hugh and his comrades who perished on the Western Front.

ACKNOWLEDGEMENTS

The author is indebted to Lieutenant Colonel Angus Fairrie, Honorary Curator of The Regimental Museum at Fort George who kindly provided access to the following:

The original *War Diary* of the 5th Battalion The Queen's Own Cameron Highlanders for 1917;
The typed *War Diary* of the 7th Battalion The Queen's Own Cameron Highlanders for 1915;
The Recruiting Register for Lochiel's Camerons 1914;
Historical Records of The Queen's Own Cameron Highlanders Vol IV, W Blackwood and Sons Ltd 1931.

Lieutenant Colonel Fairrie also gave permission to reproduce the following:

Extracts from *Yuletide Greetings from the Cameron Highlanders: In the field Christmas 1918* which was designed in the field by Albert Lemmon;
A postcard copy of a watercolour painting of *The Inverness Militia at Camp, Cameron Barracks, Inverness*, by Major R A Wymer, 3rd Camerons 1907;
A sepia photograph of a painting by Joseph Gray of the Battle of Loos at Hill 70 on display at The Regimental Museum at Fort George.

Permission to reproduce photographs was also gratefully received from the following: J Gordon Mcintyre, Clifton House Nairn; Mrs Joyce MacDougall, Kilchrenan; Mrs Helen Taylor, Ardeonaig; and Arthritis Care.

The assistance of the archivist at The University of Glasgow and the archivist for Stirling Council is much appreciated.

The author is also grateful to Dr Diana M Henderson, Research Director of the Scots at War Trust, for writing a Foreword for the book.

NOTES ON CONTRIBUTORS

Captain Hugh Mann, an Arts graduate of the University of Glasgow, was a student of Divinity at the United Free Church College in Glasgow prior to joining the Cameron Highlanders in October 1914. Injuries received at the Battle of Passchendaele on 12 October 1917 led to his death in a military hospital at Le Tréport on the Normandy coast a month later. The greater part of the letters included in this book were written by Hugh.

Jessie Mann, née Reid, was a first year Arts student at the University of Glasgow prior to the outbreak of the First World War and her marriage to Hugh. The last eight letters written by Jessie to Hugh were returned to her after his death. These, and letters from Jessie to her parents as Hugh fights for his life, form the latter part of this book.

Hector Hetherington (later Sir Hector) married Jessie's older sister Alison in 1914. He was latterly Principal and Vice-Chancellor of The University of Glasgow from 1936 to 1961. Letters written by both Hector and Jessie to Jessie's father in December 1914 are included in Part II.

Dr Diana M Henderson, the author of the Foreword, is Research Director of the Scots at War Trust and the author of a number of books on military history.

Bríd Hetherington, a teacher and college lecturer for many years in Scotland and abroad, comes from Dublin and is daughter-in-law to the late Scott Hetherington, elder son of Hector and Alison Hetherington. She is author of the narrative and editor of *Under the Shadow*.

FOREWORD

Under the Shadow is a sad but inspiring story worthy of Grand Opera. A Romeo and Juliet tale of young love, passion, guilt, prejudice, war and death. But this is not Verdi or Shakespeare, it is the Camerons and Shettleston, and as these letters so ably testify, it is true.

Typical of thousands of young men at the time, Hugh Mann fell in love. Her name was Jessie. They were both young, attractive, articulate and intelligent. They were however middle class and when Jessie became pregnant the full force of Scottish middle class prejudice and hypocrisy of that time was brought to bear on them. Amongst all the letters, that of Jessie's brother in law, Hector Hetherington, is probably the most telling in its sharp criticism of these attitudes.

The letters themselves are testimony to a different age. Today not only would the reaction be different, but the letters themselves would not exist, and such words as there were would probably be said over the telephone. It is clear from the letters that these are two intelligent, if naïve, young people well able to express themselves, but unable or unwilling to break the bonds of family.

Set against the background of this story, the whole business of conducting a war appears all the more stark. But war is stark, and today the realities of battle do not fit easily into the same box as the rest of our emotions. So distant are we now from these realities that we have conveniently forgotten the millions who survived, the joy, relief and pride of victory, the fun, the adrenalin and the good times, some of which Hugh touches on.

In the context of events, the war is a delay and a good excuse for not facing up to a real situation. In this respect Hugh's death is virtually inevitable. In Verdi however, the hero gets up from his deathbed to take the curtain calls.

These treasured letters, long preserved by an elderly lady, are a story on many levels and they have a value that was never anticipated by the young people who wrote them. In making them available Bríd Hetherington has rendered a service to history, to literature and to love.

Dr Diana M Henderson
Edinburgh 1999
Research Director, Scots at War Trust

CONTENTS

Hugh and Jessie Mann with their young son Duncan Cameron (Micky) circa September 1917

INTRODUCTION

Under the Shadow is the story of a young couple engulfed in a long and brutal war, a war which led to the mobilisation of 65,038,810 men worldwide, 8,020,780 of whom lost their lives. But the cost in terms of human suffering in The Great War extended way beyond this figure. Nearly a third of those who took up arms, 21,228,813 in all, were wounded. Many were left maimed for life or had their lives cut short. In over four years of war, men of every nationality, colour and creed faced shells, bullets, bombs and torpedoes. Some were gassed and quickly died of drowning as fluid filled their lungs. Weak and injured men succumbed to gangrene, dysentery or other illness. Among the soldiers of the British Empire alone over three thousand received death-sentences from their own masters for desertion, cowardice, murder, mutiny or sleeping at their posts: of these, three hundred and forty-six were executed. The men at the Western Front, or at Gallipoli, or other battlefields were our fathers, grandfathers, great-grandfathers or other close relatives: very few families were left unscathed. Some were regular soldiers or members of the Territorial Army. Others responded in 1914 and 1915 to Kitchener's call to arms. Many more were conscripted.

Now as the last of the survivors leave us, and the century which endured two world wars draws to a close, the intimacy, the hopes, the tribulations, the brutality and even the novelties, challenges and exhilaration of The Great War will be fading into the annals of history. While it is all too easy to forget, the men who sacrificed their lives in a war outwith their control, should not be forgotten. The countless military burial sites in every continent remind us of untimely deaths. The Menin Gate at Ypres in Belgium, inscribed with the 54,896 names of British and Empire soldiers whose burial places in the Ypres Salient are unknown, is only one of many notable monuments commemorating those who fell in battle. Here at the Menin Gate traffic is brought to a standstill and trumpets sound The Last Post at eight o'clock every evening of the year to call on us to pause awhile and remember. "That their names may live", the epitaph boldly inscribed on The Stone of Remembrance in many military cemeteries is more than a simple prayer. It is an urgent call. On remembrance hangs our hope that, for the sake of our children and future generations, the madness of war can be kept at bay forever.

The Menin Gate at Ypres

Both Hugh and Jessie lived in Shettleston in the East End of Glasgow. Hugh Wallace Mann was "son of the manse", his father being Minister of Eastbank United Free Church in Shettleston, while Jessie Reid's father was Headmaster of Wellshot Public School, also in Shettleston. The first of Hugh's letters to Jessie is dated July 1911 when Jessie is just turning sixteen and still attending Glasgow High School. Hugh is twenty-one, and has recently graduated with an Arts Degree from The University of Glasgow. He later joins the United Free Church College in Glasgow to study for church ministry, thus following in his father's footsteps.

The depth and seriousness of Hugh's and Jessie's relationship from early days are evident in Hugh's letters and one of his preoccupations when separated from Jessie is with planning their honeymoon. The location for this great event changes as each holiday evokes fresh images of romance and perfection. Sadly, the outbreak of war in 1914 shatters any prospect of conventional celebration of nuptial bliss with their hastily arranged marriage taking place on the very day Hugh enlists with Lochiel's Camerons. Their love proves too strong to be dented by such a harsh hand of fate and neither pressure to conceal their marriage and the birth of their son, nor separation, detracts from a relationship that has left to us a very special collection of candid and lively letters. The early letters draw us into the day-to-day affairs of the young Scot who finds holidays difficult as they remove him from Jessie who is "the centre of things". Later letters take us to army training camps in Scotland and England before Hugh crosses the Channel to France and Flanders Fields. Hugh's letters unfold a tale of love and war, a true tale which puts us in touch, not only with deprivation and death, but also with the exhilaration and challenge of battle.

But that is not all. Jessie's own last letters to Hugh which were returned to her on his death, along with letters written by Jessie to her parents from the hospital at Le Tréport on the Normandy coast where Hugh spent his final days, have been preserved along with Hugh's. These place a poignant seal on their years together. But Hugh and Jessie's story did not end there. The leather case which contained the letters was also home to precious reminders of their only son, including postcards sent from his hospital bed to his grandmother in the weeks before his untimely death after a short illness in 1931 at the Glasgow Royal Infirmary. He was just sixteen years old.

Various other documents found their home in the small leather case as well as some little mementoes of Hugh's army life such as his metal pocket size, foldable, trench vanity mirror. Most moving of all perhaps was a tiny suede wallet about one and a half inches square containing photos of Jessie and their little boy at their hideaway home, the schoolhouse at Ardeonaig on Loch Tay: photos small enough for Hugh to carry in trenches and in battle. The suede wallet also harboured a miniature folded silk Union Flag.

As many of Hugh's letters are undated, it took many hours of painstaking detective work to place them in exact chronological order. Sometimes the placing had to be decided by matching paper or ink when the content offered no clues. Some of the letters are very fragile and faint, especially those written at the Western Front on flimsy paper and in pencil; others are still fresh and crisp. Apart from omitting punctuation in addresses and salutations and the use of italics, the letters have been presented authentically. Hugh wrote even the most hurried of notes with remarkable accuracy and hardly ever scored out a word. His use of hyphens in words such as "to-night" or "to-gether", deliberate misspellings in order to imitate an accent and an abundance of dashes and commas have been faithfully retained.

Because of censorship at the Front, Hugh was unable in his letters to give any indication of his whereabouts, billets or trenches. However, the movements and locations of Hugh's battalion have been traced from the battalion's daily records which were kindly made available by Lieutenant Colonel Angus Fairrie, Curator of the Regimental Museum at Fort George near Inverness. Relevant information has been presented in introductions to the sections and chapters of this book in order to place the letters in their military, social or geographical context without causing too much disruption to the flow of the letters.

The title "Under the Shadow" is Hugh's. In July 1914 he reads through letters "full of pain and heartening" written to him by Jessie from Pirnmill following his father's death the previous year. "It comes to me," he writes, "that you and I made our best friendship under the shadow. Some day we shall read them over together and perhaps we shall find, as I did, that our eyes grow full of unashamed tears." Sadly, those "unashamed tears" were Jessie's alone. Thanks to Jessie however, it is now our turn to read and perhaps shed a tear or two. Unfortunately the fate of Jessie's letters to Hugh is not known with the exception of the last few, included in this collection, which Hugh was not to read and which were returned to Jessie after his death. Their "best friendship" had indeed been formed "under the shadow".

Those who remember Jessie remember her cheerfulness and her smile. By publishing the letters which she guarded so dearly until her death in 1976 we would hope to celebrate Jessie and Hugh's friendship, their intimacy, their love, laughter and pain. Moreover, the fortitude of Jessie and the many millions who were left widowed, fatherless, brotherless or friendless as loved ones were slaughtered, wounded, or maimed for life must also be celebrated. But above all, by reading these letters, we will remember Hugh himself and the many thousands who fought on in the mud of Flanders with little or no hope of survival: the men who did not live to see Armistice Day eighty years ago.

PART I

Scotland: July 1911 - October 1914

Hugh & Jessie, March 1914

Hugh Wallace Mann graduated with an Arts Degree from the University of Glasgow on the 20 June 1911 where he had studied from 1908. During his three undergraduate years he covered a wide range of subjects including Moral and Political Philosophy, Political and Social Economy, Geography, Latin, Greek and English. His study of English and the Classics perhaps accounts for the ease and accuracy with which he writes. Letters are often enlivened by forays into Latin, Greek and French. There are also Biblical and rhetorical overtones, often humorous, undoubtedly absorbed growing up in a manse but perhaps also the result of his own studies for church ministry which began in the autumn of 1911 at the United Free Church College in Glasgow. It was then, as a Student Missionary, that he became involved in both pastoral work and preaching. From April 1913 until he joined the Queen's Own Cameron Highlanders, Hugh assisted the Rev Hugh Mair at the now demolished Wellpark United Free Church at 165 Duke Street in Glasgow. Although Hugh had been born in Langholm in the Scottish Borders he moved to Shettleston in Glasgow when his father became Minister of Eastbank United Free Church in 1901.

It is not clear when Hugh's friendship with Jessie began. In the teasingly pompous first letter of this collection he refers to their 'ancient friendship'. Perhaps he is being facetious but it is also possible that they had known each other for some time. Arnold, Jessie's brother, was a friend of Hugh's and graduated from Glasgow University at the same ceremony as Hugh, and it may be that Hugh came to know Jessie through Arnold at the Reid family home or on the Shettleston to Glasgow train journeys to their respective places of learning.

In the summer of 1911 Jessie was just sixteen and a pupil at Glasgow High School for Girls. A school report for 1911/12 describes her as "most intelligent" and "a pupil of great promise". She passed English and Mathematics at Higher Grade in 1913 after which she matriculated at Glasgow University to study for an Arts degree with Latin and Mathematics in her first year. Jessie was the fourth of seven children of William and Jessie Reid (née Hunter). William Reid had been Headmaster of Airth Public School, and later Alva Public School, before becoming Headmaster of Wellshot School in Shettleston in 1904. In 1911 he took over at the helm of Eastbank Academy in Shettleston and within a few years he had transformed the Academy from a three-year secondary to a full secondary school. A staunch supporter of the established church in Scotland, The Church of Scotland, he became Session Clerk in Shettleston Parish Church and representative elder in the Presbytery of Glasgow.

Chapter 1

"I suppose it will be a few years before we set out together, but it will be, and that settled we must just go ahead as best we may."

Hugh's early letters to Jessie introduce a young man, recently graduated, filled with vitality, fun, and above all, love for Jessie. The first letter is sent to Jessie on the Isle of Arran in the Firth of Clyde where Jessie's family spent the month of July every year. Later Hugh writes from Brodick on Arran to Jessie in Glasgow. A number of these early letters are addressed from Nairn, a town on the Moray Firth east of Inverness. Lovat Lodge in Nairn had been a family home until the late thirties but it is currently a hotel owned by *Arthritis Care,* while Clifton House, built in 1873 and now a stylish hotel, would also have been a private dwelling at the time of Hugh's visit. As Hugh's father came from Nairn, it is possible that Hugh was staying with relatives at the time of writing.

Hugh frequently addresses Jessie as K or Kiddie in these first letters in recognition of their age difference perhaps, but as their relationship develops he abandons this form of address completely.

Hugh's graduation at The University of Glasgow 1911

9 Mansion House Drive
Shettleston NB
10th July 1911

My dearest *Je-hessie*

Thank you very much for the beautiful diary, which I duly received and dutifully concealed from my parents. Most of the orthography is in your deplorable writing, and my sole object in writing you is to correct a few of the most vital and elementary points of spelling and grammar.

Your opinion on the spelling "suspender" (incidentally not a lady like subject) differs considerably from the late Dr. Johnson, a very worthy man - of whom you may have heard me speak. Again what you honour me by calling our "masterpiece" ought not to be spelt "masterpeace". Not my dear Jessie, because the one is not as good as the other - but simply because the former is more usual and we do live in a world of convention.

The sentiments are admirable and I shall have pleasure in continuing the tome where you left off - I may not, of course be quite so candid. Let me have some more of your work. Though you are still young your style shows some distinction, and no one would be happier than I were you to start under my auspices a career which may lead you to Westminster or the gallows. My own opinion on this latter point I reserve, as it is far from me to say anything which might bring to a premature conclusion our ancient friendship.

Meantime, dear madam, with as much love as you can collect from Mamie, I remain,

Your obedient, humble servant,

Hugh Wallace Mann

(No address nor date but likely to be December 1911)

Cherie

I'm glad to know your throat is better. Alison[1] said in the train this morning that you were taking something, and tho' I was pretending to swot like blazes, I heard that all right. So you can imagine what a pleasant day I've spent. I only came up to-night to get first-hand evidence.

The exam was pretty easy, and if I don't get 70% I'll stop writing exams at all. On the other hand to-morrow will be a crusher. I'm mighty glad you are coming. Quite apart from any disappointment to me, I know it would have been a beastly one to you, and I was sorriest at that prospect. I have decided what to give you for X'mas - a bottle of - no, you're wrong - I'm *sorray* - only of scent - Rhine violets for preference. Will that suit your dear little ladyship?

Isn't it nice sitting here alone with you about ten yards away; and yet you might be as many miles. I have a bit of a cold yet, but it's done its *darnedest,* and it is well nigh spent, like the day. I have given it every chance, for I played footer after the exam this morning till the sweat ran into my eyes, and then walked straight down to Craig's without a hat. Coddling a cold's no good. It's got to be shamed out. I got A for Denrey's essay. He said it was good, careful(!) work. I'm still on this blamed 'I' tack! My lips have gone rotten like yours - overwork, I expect - that is, of the lips.

By the way, have I mentioned that it is rather a bad day? My guv'nor is sitting before a big fire with a plaid round his knees cursing the day he was born. He has to go out to-night, and one would think he had been ordered to find the South Pole at a penalty of eternal perdition if he didn't. I was sorry not to be able to oblige Stuart Kinloch last night. He is such a good sort. But partly I funked it, and partly I wanted to be somewhere else on Thursday night. That 'somewhere else' I can safely leave to your prosaic imagination. We shall have to be mighty careful of you to-morrow, because if you are the worse of it, we may have trouble in repeating the experiment. So we're going to bob seats in La Scala, and we're not going to stand at the Kings. We'll try the early doors Upper Circle just on 6.30, and I fancy we'll get in somewhere.

If you had been down here, I was going to trespass on your good-nature to the extent of asking you to read Corinthians again. But I'll just have to buckle to, and do the beastly bilge myself. Hence, idle refining! I can see daddy Orr correcting my exam-paper to-night, and repeating to himself the words of that picturesque old ballad, 'For I've got you and you've got me, so everything's all *rai-ight'*. But I prefer to keep them for our own special application.

Dare I send endearments in this John Bulline Open Letter? If you get too fed up, write back. I won't be too busy to read it, I guess.

δουλος σου*

*Your slave

(No address nor date)

Dear K[2]

I'm sorry if I had you waked, and it's stinking that you have toothache. Cheer O, little one. À *demain.* My own eyes are slipping close, but I'll have to go on till about one o'clock to get through. Pity me, *et pensez de moi.* Good-night, Jess. I'm just going off. I wish you could hand over your toothache to me. I would positively enjoy having it, if I knew it was saving you pain.

Good-night, ownest own.

Lovat Lodge

Nairn

2nd January 1912

Dear Jess

I suppose you ought to have been asleep, but then if you had, I should not have known what you were thinking; and then how much poorer I should have been. Are you lonely, dear? So am I, in the midst of a crowd. The days are long. This is only Thursday. We put in a most energetic day. We had another *cousinly* foursome this morning. Then a walk in the afternoon followed by a scratch hockey match on the lawn, and here I am sitting before the fire alone. The others have all gone out, but I pled weariness and letters to write. You will give me a kiss in thought, when I tell you that at 5.50 I have only smoked three cigarettes to-day. Whose influence is that? Indeed dear, it is easy to slip into a conception of marriage by which it becomes a *propagatorium*. But there is a much truer spiritual side. I should never marry you if I could possibly do without you - and I should never ask you to marry me if you could get along without me. But we can't, dear - and there it is. It's awful to think of how much I'll lean on you, Jess, but you'll not mind it, if I know the least thing about your brave wee soul. I suppose it will be a few years before we set out together, but it will be, and that settled we must just go ahead as best we may.

I take you in my arms, Kiddie.

Yours ever and ever, H

5th January 1912

Dear K

I haven't heard from you for ages now. I suppose because you are in *Tilly*[3]. I guess you'll be home before this arrives though. I do hope you have had a decent jolly time, for no one deserves it more than you, little one. I put your letters under my pillow one night, and slept so. I dreamt very weird things, but the only one I remember now is that papa took my proposal as a matter of course and made one of his jokes about it. Let's hope it may be prophetic. You may know how I miss you, Kiddie, when I tell you solemnly that I have smoked a 20 box of *'Three Castles'* in 3 days. Sober truth! It gives me a kind of savage pleasure to deny myself because you asked me to do it. Truth is, too, that I'm ever so much better. I'm really as fit as a fiddle now, and I am sure I can stick out next term. I was just as sure I couldn't a fortnight ago. Jess, I've been mooning about here, deciding what a fine background everything would make if I could get fixing the foreground to suit my exquisite taste. I fancy you could guess at that foreground. Kiddie, the time's going past somehow. Only five more days and I shall see you. Will I pick you up in my arms before them all? I will if you like. I was up at the station yesterday and I envied the south express. I sent a kiss by it to you. I hope it was delivered.

Mater was trying to persuade me to cut supper out at your place. She says I'm trespassing on your kindness. But you see, dear, I've no pride where you are concerned, only need. A starving man is seldom proud. He forgets everything but his want. *Voilà!* Little Jess, I'm so impotent. I want to do something, but I can't get to you. My love, my love, Jess. Kiddie, our cure for this sort of thing is humour, if you remember. But I've got none away from you either. Good-night darling sweetheart. I press you to me, dear. H

28th 8 pm

K dear

I looked long for it. Have you ever considered the infinite attractions of the great play *"Hamlet"* staged with the Prince of Denmark left in his dressing-room? I have been playing sister Anne to the local man of letters thrice daily after meals. You have a confiding way of sneaking into a fellow's heart. I earnestly trust no other male experiences the sensation - for behold and know that the *Lord thy God is a jealous God.* Well dear, what can one say? Except possibly that I am completely unsettled and miserable. One laughs - Lord, yes, of course - one's inmost innards aren't a public peep-show - but - you say you think. Kiddie, you go about with me all the blessed time. It's distinctly irritating, because your shadow is mighty elusive - I try to fix you as you were at a time. But some other phantom appearance of yours creeps in, and the image is blurred: follows "a cry and a sigh and a sick longing." In truth I can't see my way very far. How is this winter to pass? I guessed it would be bad - but I can't seem to get you to myself at all. We will allow ourselves about one picture-house a fortnight - no more. I'm not going to have you talked about by a pack of damned scandal mongers. *Excusez,* but I know them and their type. Then there is the 8.27. I've a nine o'clock class, praise God.

Kid, I came home Sunday night just to be a few miles nearer you. True, I assure you. Mad, of course, perfectly mad, but drop a tear on his tomb for he died of love. Amn't I simply raving, but I'm so glad to get your letter that I could stand the King a drink. I didn't say much about London and so forth, but my point of view all the time was a double one. I'll show Kid this, "She mustn't see that". I have it all cut and dried. I break the thrilling news to you. We are going to London for our honeymoon - with the consent of the Princess always of course.

I am sitting alone in the study. I keep thinking that if I but had you here, we could together face up to things. I am afraid to look at the years, Kid, that's the truth of it. Why should we waste the best years of our lives waiting and wearying - there is no answer to that delightful conundrum. I spent Sunday afternoon looking at a fire - the place would be really quite decent - I peopled it with you and others. It made one sad. You will feel the same, I guess. It's a rum sort of world. Dash, tho' Kid, I'm giving us both the blues. We'll win through somehow to our City o' Dreams. I've been aching for Saturday and it's only Wednesday. Come home early, for my sake. I'll be up likely in the afternoon. Arnold[4] and I are going to some beastly fireworks on Glasgow Green at night - Comet celebration or something. If you're not tired ask to come too and I'll back you up - we might get a stray minute to ourselves.

"Have I been playing tennis?" There is a weird attraction about an empty nest. Yes, I've been playing tennis using your racket with your name on it, doubtless carved by your hands; and I fancy Arnold can't quite understand why I handle the thing so reverently. I fear at this point I'm going to rhapsodize like an amorous shop-walker. If you don't like it, skip. Kid, I want you so badly. I want to take you in these cylindrical extensions one terms arms. I want to hold you close, and closer, to look into your eyes - they take such a tight hold of me these eyes of yours - and to kiss you, Kid, till I have to order your little heart to stop thump-thumping. Do you catch my sort of madness in this linguistic Bedlam? You have become so much part of me that I miss you with a physical pain. When you come near, my hands tremble - absolutely and truly - I now stop talking like this - I have made myself into what we call a *Silly Auss*. But it is to you, so it don't matter. You asked me to write you a satisfying letter. If this doesn't satisfy you - I can't ever or at all, for I have given you all I have, am, or hope to be - to wit, that bundle of tissues locally known as H. Wallace Mann. I post this at once - that you may write again. Pity a man dying of thirst and send him water - the only water that will avail. Write soon Kid, and much, much.

Yours simply,

Hugh

If you think anyone might see this, burn it at once. I have read it over and I am ashamed of my ravings. Mercifully I could write like this to one person only.

(The following would appear to have been written about this time. The first page is missing but the reference to 'Ascog' indicates that it was written on the Island of Bute in the Firth of Clyde.)

I'm wandering, old lady, but I feel better, less lonely, less objectless. I'm off to bed - there's three striking. I don't know what your ideas about religion and serious things are. I am a humble striver after the light - and - why should one be ashamed to say these things? I always stick a little piece in about "my little Kiddie" when I'm finishing my day's account. I reckon that whoever is in charge up there will understand, will separate the dross from the good stuff in me and in you, and will bring us together in His own good time. I don't mean to sermonize, old lady. I'm off to bed. Good-night, and my own lassie, my dear, good-night.

It's a grand morning and I'm going to walk three healthy miles to church. If I could tuck your arm under mine and set off, it would be better. But χρονος φευγει.* Six good miles before dinner. Out in 43 minutes, in 39 - that's good going. Enough to knock the devil out of me. I heard a pal of mine, Wilson, preach. I'm just off to meet him and bring him to have tea with me. I'm mighty glad of the company. I was asked to the Manse for dinner - four girls and a boy - 23, 20, 19, 17, 15 - good selection - and I declined!!! You can guess what a slight temptation it was to me, when there's a 'you'.

7.30 p.m. and I have walked 18 miles. I went back to Ascog for Wilson in the afternoon, brought him in with me to tea, and walked back with him. I must confess that I am terribly *'wabbit'*, in your own dear idiom, but I am too tired to worry and all is *weel*. In a way I hope Arnold isn't coming down as I shall see you the sooner. But I'm almost worried about what to do. Laugh as you will. I am a nuisance coming to your house every night - perhaps not to you, but, however kind and loveable your people are to me I can't help feeling that I am very often *de trop* and a bore. You see I am really and sincerely shy. I don't think you believe that, but it's true. However we shall see how things turn out. Kid I'm too *fagged* body and soul to write more. I can think of nothing but 'I love you'. I'm away from you: I'll soon be with you.

Hugh

* *Time flies.*

Grand Hotel du Nord (what!)

Boulogne

14th August 1912

Dear K

Methinks in a rash moment I promised to write you so *voilà*! - which summarises very concisely the atmosphere round about here. Hamburg was going to be too expensive so we decided upon this place. We crossed yesterday in a small gale and we are in very comfortable quarters. I have caught myself wishing you were over, as the beastly jargon has tripped me up several times. I went into a barber's shop this morning, and asked in my best French for a shave, whereupon the silly ass got hold of my boots in order to get in to my corns to cut them. The annoying thing was that he could speak English quite decently. We were in the Casino last night. I didn't lose anything as I didn't bet - (not by the way, on principle, but in case I lost my little all). Then we found ourselves at a comic opera. But the heat and the jaw and other things drove us out in ten minutes. To-night we are going to the Kursaal, the local music-hall. I have been drinking half a bottle of light wine per meal. I got quite giddy at first, but I'm hardened now. There's too much "I" about this blamed epistle. *Excusez-moi!*

Arnold told me you were at Brodick with the Kinlochs. I hope you have a good time. No, that sounds small. I hope you have a real, rattling good time. I expect to be back Wednesday or Thursday of next week.

Yours

Lovat Lodge

Nairn

Tuesday December 31st 1912

Dearest K

I have had no letter from you yet, but I feel like writing you. I'm dead fed up. In other words, I need you horribly. I had a very strenuous week-end in Langholm - two services and the Sunday School. Then there was a nervous strain. The wee Kirk was crammed at night. The whole blessed Session and Managers filed into the vestry afterwards and said some very kind things. So altogether it was mighty trying. There was that beastly early start - at quarter past six. We weren't in Nairn till 9.20. Oh that blessed Highland line! I found Tim [5] tremendously well, so well that he whacked me at golf this morning. By the way the mater thinks I'm on my last legs - pale and thin - Lord!!! This place is all right, but - there are two cousins of mine staying with us. A confounded nuisance! Excuse the *hand o'write*. Explanation is that I've just finished a too-hard game of football. I can't write any more, as they are wondering what I'm at. All my love, my very own lassie.

Your

H(usband)

Lovat Lodge, Nairn

Lovat Lodge
Nairn
1st January 1913

Sweetheart

A Happy New Year. That was a rather scrappy little note I sent you yesterday, but I was very tired. I find that I am not in form for the severely physical day they put in here. We played a foursome this morning with my cousins. The links are extra fine.

I got your letter, little one, by this morning's mail. Jolly glad I was to get it, dear. Of course go to *Tilly;* when did I ever wish to stop your enjoyment of life? Give my regards to Mamie, if you remember, a thing that slipped your memory last time. I am mighty glad to hear your cold is on the move. It makes things much cheerier to know that you are not seedy or anything. Myself I am fairly decent - cold nearly away. Wasn't it too bad - that fellow in Langholm not merely let me off without the fee - he didn't even give me expenses. I dropped about fifteen bob on the thing. It's hard luck to be swindled that way without any redress; for I would cut my hand off before I asked him for a penny. Haven't met any girls here at all and I'm not putting on mourning. Besides there aren't any girls in the world: there's only one, and I've collected her. It's boring, this place. I wouldn't say to any one but you, but I feel desperately out of key with the atmosphere. They say I'm moody and quiet. It's all true, but they don't know why, and I do. I keep thinking that the place would be a perfect Paradise if you were up - but as it is the Paradise holds no attractions for me. Wee Jess, I love you most *desprit.* I'm sorry you don't approve of the way I fold clothes, but I will be more than charmed to take lessons from you. The fees will be kisses and if you don't feel satisfied you can return them.

I'm not smoking very many "cigarrettes" (sic), but if you say I'll cut down still further. Oh! What you say when Arnold comes in! Here's the mater, wanting to know to whom I write. Answers the dutiful son, "Mind your damned business." Sorry, sorry.

Keep writing Jess darling. Only yours,

Hugh

Lovat Lodge
Nairn
8th January 1913

This is a devil of a pen.

My darling lassie

I got your letter this morning, and mighty glad I was to see it. Do you know you left me six mortal days without a word? I have no doubt that as usual you will have a perfect excuse, but that doesn't really soothe my anxiety. However, let it go. I'm glad you had a decent time at Tilly. Arnold is playing up well. He is a real sport. But I wouldn't blame him, if with the knowledge of my confounded follies that he has, he refused to help at all. He is another individual who will be welcome at our joint fireside. I feel wretched that you are at school, and I am still on holiday. It isn't fair that the little one should have the heavy end of the stick; but what can one do?

You aren't nice enough over the cigs. You might have sweetened more. I only had <u>five</u> yesterday. Today it is 11.30 and I haven't had one yet! I am beastly like a small boy to the extent that when I am good I love to be told so.

This will be my last note to you from here. If I've any luck I'll get one yet from you. I'll be up, not before seven. My train doesn't get to Buchanan Street till about 5.40 or so.

There is perfect weather up here, a whole stretch of whin is in bloom. It would all be tremendously happy and lovely 'were you my bride'. I have not yet started the sermon I am due to get done here. I cannot force myself to get the blamed thing on the stocks. I'm walking up to the Post Office that you may get this a day earlier.

All my love, darling. In three days I'll have you again, my sweetheart. H

9 Mansion House Drive

Shettleston NB

Bed 19th March 1913

Dear

I am nailed this time. My mater and my doctor have entered into a league to sit on my chest, and I have only had one cigarette to-day, and even that I had to steal. I was fairly rotten yesterday, and the doctor won't let me go in to my exams to-morrow. I'm not breaking my heart about that, but the beggar has stopped Cumnock too. I don't know when I'll get up, Jess darling, so this is only a *'floreas'* for your exams. The best of luck, lass of mine; I'm dead sure you'll get through. I'm feeling pretty fed up that I can't get to you. Would that my mamma asked you down to cheer me up. I need it badly. I've followed every hour yesterday and to-day wondering just where you were, and what you were doing. I'm going to try to be in the train on Monday or Tuesday, so that we can arrange for Thursday. Can you write two lines and a kiss back to me? Not much, dearest, as I know how thundering busy you are.

I'm going to ask dad for a stamp for this, and then ask him to post it for me! My own love-lass. I want you just frantically here, nobody but you, Jess. "*Je t'embrasse douce mille temps*" (not quite a literal transcription).

Girl, girl, I love you. H

Ashfield
Douglas Row
Brodick
31st March 1913

My own darling wee girl

Here we are safe and sound. My rig just now is thoroughly unconventional - *the semmit and footer shorts you wot of.* I am by no means the worst, as one man has emerald green stockings and another dashing red ones.

I had quite a decent time at Milngavie - they gave me a fire in my bedroom. I liked the church very hugely and the manse was a paradise *pour toi et moi.*

I haven't much time, as the men are clamouring for a side at football.

I salute you, oh my only love. Yours always and ever,

Hugh

All good luck, darling, in your papers.

Ashfield
Brodick
Arran
3rd April 1913

Dearest Kiddie

Sorry not to have written before. You won't think I am forgetting you, will you? Things hum so much here and one is so tired by sitting down time, that I prefer to think of you than to write. You're my only correspondent, if that is any satisfaction - even my home people have not had a card.

I have had a lot of worry over the concert to-morrow night. The programme was thin enough, and now my throat has absolutely crocked with yelling and a touch of cold, so I have to cut myself out.

I'm coming up on Saturday afternoon but I have to go to see my future session clerk at Wellpark in the evening so I can't get up. Hope to see you Monday though.

All my love and a lot more. Your boy, H

9 Mansion House Drive
Shettleston NB
21st April 1913

My darling Jess

Ye wee divil ye! You would chaff me about this *** measles business would you? I have been cursing my head off over it. For you see I don't feel anything but very well, and the only risk is that of infection to other people. By the way, if you are afraid of it, you'd best slip this in the fire now. I was in a fearful state on Thursday night. I got your letter by the afternoon post, and Arnold couldn't get my card till Friday morning. I couldn't even write to you. The way I did was the only thing I could think of. And I pictured poor little you waiting for the third cruel night. My dear, I was coming up on the Wednesday night about half past eight, when my visiting was done. But I had such an obvious dose of something that I daren't, for love of you, risk it. I was two long days lying on my back thinking of you, girl in all the settings I've seen you in, since you came to me.

Jess dear, we are going to be desperately happy, I am sure of that. If the steak is burnt to a cinder, I shall dine off you and your bonnie eyes. And if you, with perfect justice lose your rag about something I have done, I shall pull you into my arms, and solemnly say 'Diddums', or something equally inane; which you nevertheless will receive as the profoundest wisdom. What skittles I talk, Jess, don't I? I had Arnold for nearly four hours last night. How I clung to that lad's conversation! I switched him round as often as I could to you, and he was very obliging. I think he won't curse if I become his brother by marriage. We have almost arranged it that I am to spend some time with him at Dulnain in June - when I get my holidays. I was wondering if you could get up at the same time. I could travel with you to protect you on the journey. There are perfect walks at the place. Does it attract you, sweetheart of mine? Then Arnold was asking me about July, and suggesting Pirnmill. So that may come off.

I meant to come up to-night, but it's too dangerous for the youngsters. I think you are home early to-morrow. I might come up in the afternoon and take you for a walk - unless you're *feart* for infection. All my love, darling, every bit of it.

Yours very *lonelily* and lovingly,

Hugh

9 Mansion House Drive

Just to scribble a wee line, dear, to say thanks. I'm all better now, just not strong, but I'm coming up to-morrow night even if I can't get to College.

Love, sweetheart.

Your H

9 Mansion House Drive

29th April 1913

My dearest lass

This is rotten! I went into town yesterday afternoon, and swithered about trying to get you at 4.2. But, tho' you don't believe it, I am shy, and I was afraid you would be with a whole *bang* of girls. We could have gone to that quiet little De Luxe Theatre, and had two hours to-gether. But, as I say, I *funked* it at the last moment. I am desperate to see you, dear. I am a thousand miles in the dumps, and I sometimes think we shall never come to our desire. Will you meet me at the entrance to Charing X upstairs on Wednesday afternoon when you have finished tennis - say 3.30 - and we can go off for an hour or so to the pictures? If you can't turn up, never heed writing. I'll just come on the chance of getting you, and if it doesn't come off, it can't be helped.

My bonnie girl, often you seem to come very near me, and I can get along. But whiles I can't reach you at all, and that's pretty bad. I think of you so often, dear heart, and every night I send you a kiss before I sleep. Don't laugh, dear, at the cynical and somewhat *blasé* youth you used to know, talking like a moon-struck idiot. It is you who are solely to blame; it is I who am *soully* to blame. Rotten joke, old lady - like most of them - but then they are between ourselves (very much so).

Tim will be home in a handful of hours, but I can't meet him. I will be visiting all afternoon and evening. I get rather tired of it, not so much mentally as physically. These overheated, foul-smelling places rather feed me up. All my love, my own girl, and try to be there.

Yours only and ever, H

Clifton House, Nairn, circa 1911

Clifton House
Nairn NB
Telephone 3A
30th May 1913

Dearest Jess

The merest line to indicate that the deluge of correspondence has begun. I got here safely, tho' Tim was through the fright of his life. Our train was signalled into Nairn platform and there was a cattle-truck standing on the same line. Tim was nearly frantic when he saw our train in the distance tearing along. He got the station-master and tore down the line with a red flag, and managed to stop the train just in time. It must have been like a cinematograph film. Tim's feelings were indescribable when I stepped out of the very front carriage. I couldn't understand at first why he greeted me so effusively.

I saw dear old Arnold at Broomhill. I think we were both glad to see each other. There are too many people here for my taste - not *holidayie* enough. It's not a bit like the little bungalow you and I are to occupy some day - eh lass?

I am hurried just now, so I'll have to chuck. Remember ten o'clock! Oh, Tim sends his love to his little grown-up sister-in-law. You may accept it! All my love darling.

Yours,

Hugh

I'm enclosing this in a note to your dad because some one is to post this whom I do not know.

Clifton House

Nairn NB

1st June 1913

My own Jess

Here *nous sommes rursus*! This is Sunday morning about an hour before church, and I'm waiting for Tim to come round. Rare having an idle Sunday! Tim looks very well and strong. He seems to be fit for no end of exercise. Yesterday we tried to golf in the morning. It was a lovely day, but there was a tearing gale from the west, and we couldn't play for the clouds of sand. I drove a ball into the sea, and despite the agonised protests of Tim, who feared for his dignity, I took off my shoes and socks, and waded for it. Occasionally Tim shows a little snobbishness that worries me, but I fancy it is due to the atmosphere in which he lives. He will be all right when he gets away from those 'lot of money, no brains' fools who go to make up about fifty per cent of the Nairn population. We lay watching a cricket match in the afternoon, and at night played tennis. I'm going to tell you about that. The court is asphalt or something, and very fast. I got thirty in every game from a huge nut of a player. I hardly saw his serves, and when he got annoyed, I turned my back to escape. I actually beat him six games to five, but it was desperately exciting. I enjoyed it tremendously. I'm to get a mixed double next time, but I'm sure it won't be such fun. Giggles and footers won't improve the game any.

I got your kiss last night. Tim and I were sitting on the shore about ten. I took out my watch and found two minutes to the time. I sent Tim away for ten minutes, and turned my face south. Jess darling - I'm thinking long of your bonnie eyes. All my love, *Hertzliebe*.

Your Hugh

Nairn Golf Club

2nd June 1913

Dearest Lass

Another fine open-air day. Played golf in the morning with Tim; motor run in the afternoon; tennis in the evening; picture-house with a young lady at night. What a round of dissipation - all healthy though. Many thanks, dear, for your nice long letter. I note what you say about love-making when I come back, and I am training my muscles for a rough "wooing". So, poor little Kiddie, you'll perhaps be sorry you advised me to prepare.

Never heed if your exam results are bad. You did your best, and there is a tremendous element of luck in any exam paper. The folks here are delightful, and they are bent on giving me a good time. I'm looking about for our bungalow; I have my eye on a beauty and whenever it comes into the market I shall snap it up. And so you are still in love with my ungainly person. There is a little lass here, niece of the people with whom I am staying, and she keeps making eyes. Will you mind if I tell her that you exist, and that I am private property? I shan't do so unless I have to in pure self defence. Don't worry about it in any case, as she is only nineteen, and straight from a finishing school in Yorkshire. She may go to Yorkshire or any other convenient climate so far as I am concerned. I'm telling you all this, not as a matter of vanity, but because you may know that I do nothing without your knowledge, for you are the only espoused of

Your Hugh

Clifton House

Nairn NB

3rd June 1913

My own lass

This is only to be a line, because it is eleven o'clock, and I am full wearied. That business I told you of last night is over. I have skilfully avoided the *jeune femme* all day, and markedly passed her in the High Street, so *voilà, c'est fini!* Not without regret on my part, though, for you know I like girls, if they will only stop at the right place.

A very strenuous day! Golf with Tim in the morning. Two sets of tennis with Tim in the afternoon. I won six two, six four. Then with Campbell - a fearful nut at night. Lost zero six, six eight. In the second game I got fifteen in every game. No letter from you, little lassie, for a while. But I know how busy you are, and that you don't forget even if you are pushed for time. Whisper in your ear - will you let me? I love you. Quaint idea, isn't it?

I'm weary to-night. I should love to have you smoothing my fur down and generally putting me to rights. All my love, sweetheart.

Clifton House
Nairn NB
4th June 1913

Dearest

Another day past! My time is full to the brim of nothing in particular, and I am very busy doing it.

Tim has strained his wrist at tennis and it is in bandages, so he cannot play just now. Golf was therefore off in the morning, so we strolled along to the harbour and watched the fishing-boats. We made an arrangement to go out to-morrow morning in a wee cobble for an hour at the ruinous sum of one bob.

In the afternoon I had two sets of tennis, which I won six two, six three. I am getting quite nutty at it, developing a screw skiffy, don't come off the ground service. I can't quite manage the back-handed strokes yet, but I am practising them hard.

Watched a cricket match at night, and finished by playing bridge up till half an hour ago. It has been a most perfect day, blazing hot and blue sky. I have rarely seen such a fine climate in this country. Hope your exams are getting on all right: I'm reckoning them as the reason for your not writing. A thousand kisses.

Your H

Clifton House
Nairn NB
6th June 1913

Dearest Jess

I got your confounded cheeky darling letter this morning. I read the French part with greater ease than the rest - so there, my young one. You are a daisy with your exam results - laziness comes home to roost in the bitter of a night.

I have had another rare day. Yesterday Tim and I risked our precious lives in a leaky old barge that pulled like a ten-ton yacht. This morning a loaf, and in the late afternoon a badminton garden party. All the youth and beauty of the town were there and the fun was dazzling. I played at the game for nine sets - from five to seven-thirty. I was told that I picked it up amazingly fast; and in truth and between ourselves I was nearly as good as anyone there latterly. It's more exciting and faster than tennis, also more sociable.

I'm leaving Nairn to-morrow at 3.50; so address after this to c/o dear Arnold. I have a most warm invitation back here next week, but I'll see what brother Arnold has to say to that.

My dear *li'l lass*, how you would enjoy being up here with me. God, if you were only here, it would be a perfect Paradiso. The folkies are desperately kind to one - by the way. I hope I haven't lost the accent by the time I come back that I may amuse you with it. I can collect an accent very quickly and I'm speaking this one like a native. You'll hear from me next from Dulnain. All my love, my bonnie, bonnie darling.

Yours,

Hugh

The drawingroom at Clifton House Hotel

Chapter 2

"Do you know the empty feeling of a letter that doesn't come?"

Dulnain Bridge near Grantown-on-Spey is a small, peaceful, scenic village about thirty miles south of Inverness. It was to this quiet haven that Arnold, Jessie's brother, who had graduated from University at the same time as Hugh and was now a student minister with the Church of Scotland, invited Hugh to spend some days. Hugh had written almost daily from Nairn and now, from Dulnain Bridge, the torrent of words continues.

Broomhill Station now owned by the
Strathspey Railway Company

Seafield Cottage
Dulnain Bridge
8th June 1913

Dear old lass

You are a marvel! It's great that you are through maths. I only hope English is the same. You will positively revel in the establishment's accounts now; we may even appoint you Church Treasurer. You little darling, you have been giving me a hefty lot of back-chat lately. Long may it continue.

Here I am up with little brother. He met me at Grantown station and came on to Broomhill. We tramped thro' the trackless wood (*vide Fenimore Cooper passim*) with my beastly heavy bags (not slang for trousers in this case) and *arrove* safe and sound at his little shanty. The parson's life is full of changes and as up and down as a lift boy's. It's a far cry from aristocratic Clifton House, with its Debrett lying on every table, to this back of beyond spot and I don't know which I like best. In any case, having sampled Dulnain, I am not going back to Nairn next week. I doubt I am cut out for a bachelor. Arnold and I sat up till two this morning chatting and smoking, and I loved it. Now if you had been in charge, there would have been orders to quit long before. So I'm not going to marry you. Understand that finally? I'm not going to marry you in order that I may get sitting up till the next morning.

I attended divine service this day, and sat at the feet of Arnold Gamaliel Reid. I played the organ, and knocked L out of it. Also I took the infants class (mixed) in his Sabbath School - a boy and a girl. I couldn't make them listen except by telling them stories - some of which I cautioned them not to repeat. I'm to take the evening service in three hours from this moment, when I propose to preach a rotten sermon. Jess, this place would be great for our honeymoon - trees, trees, trees, and hills everlasting. Colour and wind in your hair. It's great. You and I through the sweet-smelling pine-trees, green sinking moss below, and never a son of man for miles - only you and only me - what, Kiddie? There's always a sough of wind, and I fell asleep to the shishing and wakened to it. I can't just tell you it all, but I would love to show you it. I don't know how we are to put in the time here - just in the open all the time, and all the time I think of my darling wee Jess as my *li'l* missus in the midst of it. Golden days ahead girl. Let's whisper it - golden days. Cheek to mine, my lips to your ear, your hair about me - golden days, dear.

Shall I bore you with another page and become prosaic. Visions sort of fade, but not all and not altogether. George may take you to the Picture-House, after which he may accompany you to Jericho. I gave Tim your love and he says he will gather some shells at the next spring tide for you to play with - also do you like dolls with blue or brown eyes? Tim hasn't yet adapted his ideas to suit the facts. I really must get off and look at my stuff - if only for the sake of brother Arnold. Things are really charming up here - and then there's the big IF - if you were only here too. Well-a-day. Salute you, my woman.

Your lad

Dulnain
10th June 1913

Dearest Lass

10th! Isn't my holiday flying fast! I'm looking for a letter by the solitary post to-day, but I can't wait for it, as this letter goes off with the postman. We had a field day *yestre'en!* Three miles in the morning: four in the afternoon: nine at night - great walking! We are cycling in to Grantown this afternoon to visit a cousin of my guv'nor's. There is a tearing wind, and we shall have a hefty pull home. There is a cottage here which we have called 'Honeymoon House'. It is a little red-tiled place among the trees with a verandah and it looks right over the Spey to the Cairngorms beyond. We argue which of us shall occupy it first. In any case this is **the** place. You can come if you like, I'm a certainty. I'm preaching again next Sunday for

Henderson, the U.F.[6] man here - a decent, nervous soul. I meant to keep the day clear, but the sight of his plaintive features was too much for me and I offered my services. Short note this, Jess, as there ain't much to tell you. All my love.

Yours, H

Dulnain

11th June 1913

Dearest little Rotter

I haven't heard from you since I left Nairn, and if there isn't a letter soon, I'm going to propose to a very nice girl I met lately here. Then I shall be consoled for your defection. I have developed a liver this morning on account of excesses yesterday and I am snapping at poor innocent Arnold whenever he opens his mouth. It's a hell of a thing a liver! You also are getting the effects of my evil morning humour. Why don't you write? If you are dead send a wire. If not, a letter will do.

Yesterday we went into Grantown to call on some relatives of my dad's. Found them very nice people indeed. We go round cadging for teas - I think we have only had tea once in our own shanty. Then too, the suppers we have sneaked are innumerable. People are glad to feed two such handsome, godly lads if only for the sake of the daughters of the house.

We are going to climb Cairngorm one day soon, but it is a very stiff undertaking. The mists are very bad, and we have just to watch for a decent chance to get up.

Jess, girl - I hope the post is bringing a letter in half an hour. If he is not, I'm going to jump into that treacherous stream, the Spey. A kiss, darling.

Your H

Dulnain

11th June 1913

Dearest

I'm not reproaching you. If there had been a letter to-day, perhaps I would have done so: but since you have left me so long now, I know you must be so busy that you cannot write. Do you know the empty feeling of a letter that doesn't come? I am feeling very lonely and sad to-night. Jess, I shall never enjoy a holiday really till we holiday together. It's all right when one is tramping into the wind and the rain, but the afterwards before the fire is solitary-like. I think I have attained rheumatism in my right elbow - it is mighty painful even as I write, so this babbling is not without soul and body-cost. After dinner we set off to walk to Boat of Garten, five miles away through the pine-woods. We tracked along the railway most of the way as the going was easier. On the way back we got caught in a tremendous shower of savage rain - result, drenched to the 'altogether' and complete leopard-like change of spots.

The railway near Boat of Garten

These Highland hills cast a charm upon one, but it is a gloomy charm. They always remind me of the savage old God of the Old Testament with His sacrifices and blood spells. No wonder the Highland religion is even yet superstitious and stern: he draws it in with every breath of strong hill air. Jess, lass, you haven't told me whether you are getting my kisses every night. I am thinking to catch yours, as they fly on the long north trail. God send us safe together, old girl, 'cos I'm tired of playing at life alone: I want to live with you. Happy June bride! Will you? - Are you tired of my semi serio-tragico-comico nonsense? Never care! You must stand a lot as this broken-winded *blaguard's* little wife, and you just make a start by cultivating patience and reading this to the end. Jess, it's coming - I love you --- There, now you have it - and me. Heart-lass, laugh a little at my rubbish - but laugh with your love-voice: for it's only your daft, harmless and altogether loving lad.

Hugh

Dulnain

Thursday night

Dearest old lady

I feel a rotter nagging you for a letter when you were up to the neck in exams. Glad you got on so decently. The English papers were mighty stiff, and I can see myself coming an almighty cropper in them. I got two letters from you to-day - riches. You little darling, I am just wearying to see you. I'm coming home next Wednesday by the 8.3, arriving in Glasgow 2.10. I must see you the same day, so I am clearing out early for that laudable object. One is very tired to-night; walked to Carrbridge and *trained* back. We followed the banks of the Dulnain. You would have laughed had you seen Arnold and me wading the river with our trousers over our knees.

I'm writing this to-night because we are having a field-day to-morrow - to Tomintoul, away up eighteen miles among the Cairngorms. We shall cycle a bit of the way and walk the rest. We were counting up and we find that we have walked fifty eight miles since I came here - not bad for your soft laddie, eh? Arnold is more tired than I am to-night, and he has already departed for bed, whence I must soon follow him. We passed Honeymoon House to-night. I wish you could see it. Red tiles, ivy, glorious view, quiet, and snug. Jess! Dear, I'll soon be back - how I need you. I'm simply lost alone now. I've come to depend on you so much. I want you to tell you everything I'm doing and feeling and thinking. Do you mind, little wise heart? I must run, my own lassie; your noisy brother summons me to warm his back. Good-night, love.

Yours ever and ever,

Hugh

Dulnain

4 a.m. Friday

Dearest Jess

This is written as an after-thought. The facts are these - we went off to bed about twelve, and for two solid hours I tried to sleep. But it was very hot and stuffy, and brother Arnold was restless, and wife Jessie kept popping up and filling my thoughts - and sleep was the only thing I couldn't do. So at two o'clock I dressed, and threw on a dressing-gown, made my way stealthily into the parlour where I am now writing. By this time you will be convinced that you have netted a stark imbecile. Certainly the worthy landlady will have a fit when she chooses to come in.

Admire my record - ten miles Thursday, no sleep, thirty miles Friday. And the amazing thing is that I feel as awake and fit as a fiddle. This is a habit, though, of which you must cure me. It is all very well on holiday, when I am in top-notch form, but work-a-day life won't stand it. Well, old girl, I'm just going to chatter to you for the next hour or so - you don't need to read it all unless you care to. There is a piping mavis astride the window smashing all quiet with a terrific melody. If I could sing like this fellow, I might reasonably boast about it. I am afraid to match myself against him. *Prudentia sola nobilitas.* And so we love each other, lass of mine. I wonder what it means? Do you reckon that some Primal *Auctor* collected some stray dust, moulded it into two exquisite forms, breathed into it something called Life, developed it up through consciousness even to self-consciousness, placed and traced a whole history of the world and of men to this one end that you and I should come together and in the very coming glorify that Primal *Auctor?* I suppose love means that. More intimately, what does it mean to us? To me you are the central focus of my daily life - I sort of revolve round about you. When you come into a room where I am sitting, for example, I become desperately aware of you, and at once I begin to talk at you - even peacock-like to spread my tail-feathers, that you may admire - for admiration is the pure gateway to love. Queer thing, isn't it? I'm not really a conceited youth; but whenever you appear over the horizon I want frantically to become a very Adonis, a true Admirable Crichton, that you may be duly impressed. This is cold, cruel, cynical analysis, isn't it, but one feels cynical at this godless hour. In any case, it is all perfectly harmless, and rather loveable if you have the sympathetic heart to human weakness - which, by the way, is a very real thing. If you know not that now you will know it hereafter, when I have the honour to call you wife. Dear God, I wish it were now. I think I could fall on sleep with my head pillowed on your shoulder, and your warm arms round me.

Jess, it's a dashed queer world. Here are scores of married people sick to be free, and here are we, sick, sick to have each other. Queer business life. I wonder if, when we are married, we quarrel and bicker and discover that our tempers are incompatible, to adopt the society phrase for 'two damned fools'? Shall we ever long to be quit, you of me, I of you? I'm stopping to laugh here, my lass: or is it cry? *N'importe*, old lady, when the hitching comes along, I swear to you it is *ad ultimam finem vitae* - even if I have to hand over my total earnings to a violent *Hausfrau*, even if I have to sever my connexion with my Lady Nicotine, whose slave I am, so be it, Lord: for there's going to be no nonsense or jargon about incompatibility of temper or of any other discovery of asses to raise trouble between little Jess and the boy Hugh.

Old girl, do you think I'm a fearful boy? I suppose I have a trick of laughing at most things; mainly because in my philosophy most things require the tonic of a little happy laughter. And I swear to you, Jess, on this score I refuse ever to grow any older than I am now. But if it's a question of facing and shouldering responsibility I'm not altogether the boy. One has one's share of work to do in and for the world, and I'm a poor fly if laughter of a shallow sort creeps in there. Does it, lass? Perhaps you hear me too much laugh at everything, even my own work. But I fancy your keen eyes have seen more than that. Perchance I merely flatter myself; perchance I flatter you; I do not think so though. Jess, my dear love, I have fallen on a mood of blind adoration. It is a case of *'Adeste, fideles, venite adoremus dominum'* only this time *'dominam'!* Often I can barely credit it, that you with your bonnie face, and winsome ways, have given yourself to me - are mine, then I think of you as you stand looking up at me, in my arms, and I know it must be true - but I wonder why - and there, just there, I stop - for I never can snatch back an answer.

My own Jess-girl, I'm aching to meet the liar who says he is happier than I am - I'll crush his teeth to his toes. Well, old lady, here am I at the end of my *haverings*. May heaven see you safe through them! I wish to the deuce the landlady would get up, that she might manufacture for my *behoof* a cup of tea. My digestion is to me what his heel was to Achilles, and this type of performance touches my tummy first. The dame *du maison* is an elderly spinster, so if I wakened her by popping my head round her door, she would instantly go into rabid hysteria. I think I'll let nature do the dirty work and open her eyes. I must slip in and see if brother Arnold is sleeping. There may be some amusement to be obtained by rousing him from his happy dreams and listening. He can be real eloquent at times. Have you stuck it thus far? Ah well, it is only the *blethering* of your laddie.

Dulnain

Sunday 15th

Dear old lady

This is my last effusion. I have been preaching again this morning for the U.F man - it was very hot. The temperature is up near ninety. Things are looking most lovely. We are cycling up to Nairn to-morrow to see Tim. Glad you got on so well in those exams. I'll hear all about them in two days. I'm sorry in a way to leave my holidays behind when every one else is just thinking of going off - but I'll get back to you anyhow. It's too hot to write. All my love. H

Dulnain Bridge

Chapter 3

"I'm thinking a lovely picture of you wandering helpless and heedless round the clachan, squealing squally kittywawks in a shrill treble at the prospect of my advent."

Soon after Hugh's return to Glasgow, Jessie and her family move to the Isle of Arran for their annual holiday. They stay at Farm House, Thunderguy, near Pirnmill, a small village on the north-west of the island looking out to the Mull of Kintyre. During their vacation on Arran the young Reids are not short of company as they are joined by some friends from across the Firth of Clyde. A letter written by Lyn C Davies[7], the boyfriend of one of Jessie's sisters, states that "Thunderguy will always have a halo of happy memories round it" even though "the crowd was always too dense to have a *tête-à-tête*". During holidays on Arran it was customary for the older girls to take turns in household management. Hugh, desperate to join Jessie for a few days, is on tenterhooks as he awaits his formal invitation to Thunderguy.

Thunderguy, Pirnmill, Isle of Arran

9 Mansion House Drive

Shettleston NB

1st July 1913

Dearest old lassie

Many rejoicings at your letter. You have broken the record for writing soon. I fancy you would only get my effusions after you had posted yours. You will have had Arnold and young Stewart by the time you get this. The youth is good value, but badly spoiled. He chatters too much and there is no knowing what he will say next. He delivered himself of certain very awkward reflections and suggestions at dinner last night. He is a decent *loon* though. I have been swearing a bit. I couldn't get down with the boys to-day because of that Picture House engagement - and by the post comes a card to say that Tuesday is unsuitable - come Wednesday. Let me say it - isn't it damnable?

The old bishop went off on Sunday without saying a word to me about staying in Glasgow all July. Also, after much tribulation I have fixed up every Sunday properly, so I can get off easily on the 14th. There has been occasion to break the news here that if I was invited I would go to Pirnmill. Coolness etc, but firm attitude from Hugh and no more remarks. I wish I was with you, but it won't be so long now. I've three sermons to write this week and I haven't got one started yet - I must fly. All my love.

Yours,

Hugh

9 Mansion House Drive

2nd July 1913

Darling

This is confoundedly good weather for the coast, and confoundedly bad for the town. I go about with all the sensations of a condemned criminal. Moreover that hay fever to which I am a helpless victim has laid fast hold upon me in these latter hot days, and life is hardly worth living. I wrote a sermon yesterday, my swift mind revolving from the text to Pirnmill - the sermon is a poor one. I went in at 7 o'clock to meet Arnold and Stewart, but they foiled me. Then I went in again and got them at the 10 o'clock as they were starting north. I had to listen to a lot of *blethers,* and not one word about you. It didn't cheer me up much to hear how much time he had put in with May and how he enjoyed it. Well, well, Kiddie. I suppose it would be a rotten world if we got all we wanted.

This neighbourhood is becoming more patently deserted each day. We shall soon be alone in our glory. I had the offer yesterday of the Broomielaw Mission at £190 a year but I declined it. I think the work there would just about finish me. Don't say anything of this please; it's for your ear alone. It's too like blowing to publish this sort of thing. I've to convey that girl to La Scala this afternoon. Wouldn't I rather be lying in the boat with my head on your knee? Hector[8] seems to be shooting out his neck. Tell him one day it will maybe stay like that, and ask him how he will enjoy that. I'll break your young neck, and excise your young liver if you venture to show him our 'Order of Service'. Tell him we are too 'High Church' and ritualistic to suit his dissenting taste and leave it there. All my love, little lass.

Yours ever,

Hugh

9 Mansion House Drive

3rd July 1913

Dearest

I'm too busy this morning to write a decent note. I've a whole sermon to write before the sun goes down on my wrath. You are a good writer of letters. If I may put it so, you have a most fascinating knack of mingling news and *coos*. Isn't it funny both of us using Arnold as a telephone exchange, and apparently we both found the b- thing on strike.

Keep the new place dark till I come, and by the way, I'm still waiting for a definite invitation for the 14th. Please see that it comes up soon, as my people may make other arrangements. Tim for instance may be down any day and I don't want to be jiggered. Attend to this, like a good kid, and relieve my anxiety.

You little devil, who told you about the 'glad eye'? I'm pretty sure I didn't. Wasn't it *religiose con amore!*

A message for Hector. He says you are getting thin and pale. Of my priesthood I promote him to the rank of exorcist, so that when the wee blue *divils* get hold of you, he is to make the <u>sign</u> of a kiss (no more) over you and say *'Exorciso te in nomine Hughie'.*

Your ever, o my love, H

9 Mansion House Drive

4th July 1913

Scallywag

Wouldn't I look at you? If you are as picturesque as you suggest, it is probable that I should look at nothing else. As to throwing you over, in spite of your definite request, I have to say that I refuse absolutely to "try". I'm glad you are having such dandy weather. Hope it keeps the pot going till I come down. God help and have mercy upon one George Ross, an affable youth of eighteen - for I shan't.

You are quite right about the work. I get thro' double the quantity - and indeed it's going to be a serious problem with us in the winter - that d.d. work. Kiddie, give me a kiss - Aw, snow white (sketch of face)!

I'm thinking a lovely picture of you wandering helpless and heedless round the clachan, squealing, squally *kittywawks* in a shrill treble at the prospect of my advent.

By the way, Jess, ask Hector to cover his communications in an orthodox envelope. You know my present hours of rising, and the morning post is early. When I got up to-day, I found the guv'nor on his knees before a Greek Lexicon. This must not be - as the wasp said.

I had a young lady out to tea with me last night, took her out on the car to Baillieston, went in to the meeting, and finally landed in her parents' domicile. When I left I kissed her - it would be more accurate to say she kissed me for her age is thirteen - Had!!! I had a very poor meeting last night – twenty-nine! And I slaved to write a sermon in the heat for that. I felt mighty *cursive*.

I'm fed up! I've a slate off, and another sliding. Must be this heat. My membrane continues to be remarkably sensitive. In plain language, I'm sneezing with the weirdest effects of the most syncopated rag-time. Something like this - Air 'Mr Brown'

Chorus - Pop-Pop-Pop--Pop-Pop-Pop- Damn

Pop--Pop-Pop-Pop-Pop-Pest. Pop-Pop-

Poppop, Damn Pop.poppoppoppoppop H- etc

No wonder I'm fed up!

Is your dad fishing, and shall we row his boat, and shall he guffaw at an awkward moment? Your invitation had better hurry up. Tim will be coming down just about the time I should be clearing, and the whole thing may be jiggered. I'm really in a funk about it.

I'm off to write my third sermon this week. All my love, my Darling Kiddie,

Your affectionate Pastor

9 Mansion House Drive

5th July 1913

My Jess

You are such a good little correspondent just now. I am wondering how long this devotion will last, but far be it from the earth to quarrel with the sun-beams that warm it. I am surprised to hear that Hector is away. I had the idea that he was down for the month, and I was envying him accordingly. Where is he off to now?

You don't say anymore about your affable lad. Do you want his life spared? Jess, I can understand now how you felt in June. It's beastly lonely without you and at night when it comes to *darkling,* I get sick for you. Yesterday afternoon I was so fed up that I went away in to 'La Scala' and sat out a three hours' programme all by myself. You may judge what it was like sitting in that place alone, where I had been with you beside me, and with your hand homing mine.

I've made arrangements for Sunday week. I'm exchanging with a man in Cumbernauld, and if I didn't get back on Sunday I couldn't get down to you with the morning boat. But Bob Chisholm, good soul, is taking me up in his motor on the Sunday, and fetching me back after the Service. Isn't that champion?

What are you doing just now Jess - 10 a.m. - dipping? I have a cold (dead cold!) bath every morning. God, it was cold this day. I sprang, like Venus, full-grown and cursing from the waves. Remember me on Sunday - three services.
Your lover

> 9 Mansion House Drive
> Shettleston NB
> 7th July 1913

Dearest

I've just had Howard [9] in - the lucky beggar will see you soon. Only another week now, old, lady, and then - stars and stripes! I had a tickler of a day yesterday, but I seemed to get through all right. Tim is coming on Thursday, and that has been at once used as an argument against my going to Pirnmill - not by the guv'nor needless to say. As I remain obdurate I am now called a selfish brute or words to that effect and cold-shouldered plus the whole box of tricks. Tell me, old girl, am I a selfish brute?

Excuse this brief note. I'm just going into town - also I'm rattled.
Yours,
Hugh

> 9 Mansion House Drive
> Shettleston NB
> Tuesday

Jess you angel

You are the cleverest wee lass in all Christendom. I'm going to forgive all your blooming abuse and baiting - the rest of your news is so fine. You can go bathing with Mr. George Ross or any other confounded male who tickles your fancy, for I'll be down on Monday to *gardez-vous.* That was a bit of calm cheek about the French. I'll send you a note some day in French of such an exalted epoch that you won't be able to read it. I swear I will. Kiddie, I could just about fling myself about

- indeed I have been doing so and the scowls were hefty. But I don't give a -- *crickey.* I nearly said it that time. I asked the guv'nor if he would take my duties while I went to Pirnmill, and he said 'with pleasure'.

I went with Will Brown to the Picture-House yesterday, and he spun me a very pathetic tale about his girl in Ireland. He couldn't get anybody to chum him over in digs, and his girl was crying her eyes out. Well, Jess, I'm in love myself and I know what that kind of disappointment is - and the long and the short of it is - I have promised to go to Bangor with Brown on 4th of August (a Monday) and I will be home on the Friday or Saturday following. I hope you won't be angry, sweetheart. I was so sorry for both of them that I ran blindly into it. I'm always playing fatheaded games like that. Will you put up with me at any price? My darling we won't be long now till the *marche de nuit* comes along.

Yours, H

9 Mansion House Drive

9th July 1913

My dear Firebrand

I meant no slight upon your powers of correspondence, I do assure you. I am simply lost in admiration and delight at your regular efforts. It is almost a propaganda. You young darling - how do you enjoy chaff? Only middling, I think - (tennis!!!) There, I'll kiss it better, you cherub. As you surmise Howard will soon tumble to the state of affairs. I hope his comments, which are invariably outspoken, will not embarrass us. I like Stuart very much, but his presence will be unfortunate. Let's hope it's a rumour. I was in town yesterday from 12.30 p.m. till 11.15 p.m. I had to go in to see two of my Mission wifies off to the Saltcoats Home where by pure cheek in asking I managed to get them admitted. They were very funny. The train left at 2 o'clock, and when I got up to St. Enoch's at twenty to the hour, I found that they had been waiting since 12. Also they hadn't slept the night before for excitement. I sent them away well primed with instructions about consumption of alcohol, also with four bananas and the 'People's Friend'. Thank God I have done my duty! It's a queer life without you, Jess, and I'm not hankering after much of it. I get rather blue easily - however, there's only joy ahead just now.

Cheers! All my love,

Your boy

9 Mansion House Drive

10th July 1913

Dearest

I hope those peaches were not compote of fruit before they reached you. I was very embarrassed in the shop. The girl wanted to know too much, so I said I would write the address myself. I saw her have a *keek* at it while she was tying it on, and she smiled very sweetly as I departed.

Mother and Father are thro' in East Lothian to-day interviewing a farmer and his wife about locating Tim. I hope to goodness it comes off this time. I am having a solitary tea and then I'm off to my meeting. Did I tell you that we are having a splash on Sunday night? Jeffrey, a former missionary is to be taking the show, and as I can get back in time to go, I'm giving the choir two special anthems which I shall conduct myself. Picture me therefore doing the *Mlynarski* stunt with baggy tails and an overgrown pencil while Rome applauds.

Friday morning

I had a grand practice last night in spite of counter-attractions. I begin to think the choir likes me.

Why haven't you written for two days? Have you so many more interesting things to do? Oh! He did? And what did you say? Was that all? And did you smack his ear? You wee divil you. Only two days more.

Yours,

Hugh

Chapter 4

"My dear, I want him to know you, and I want you to love him some day as I do - and please God we shall have that joy yet."

Hugh's longed for visit to Jessie in Arran is cut short when his father is taken ill suddenly. Jessie and her family continue their holiday in Arran although her father has by this time returned to Shettleston.

9 Mansion House Drive

17th July 1913

Jess dear

I just got home an hour ago and I find things rather bad here. My dad is in bed with a high fluctuating temperature, great sickness and coughing and a colour in his spit. The doctor has ordered a nurse and she comes in an hour. It looks terribly like pneumonia with the catarrhal and *stomachie* complications. The danger is his heart. If there is a severe pneumonia strain put upon it, no one knows what will happen. Doctor is coming in again about ten to-night, and I shall buttonhole him to get his ideas. Mother is in a great fear and is quite done up. Tim is standing in like a Trojan, but I'm glad I was wired for. God knows what the end of all this will be, but dear, I can face up to whatever is coming with your love behind me. I can't find things to tell you how you cheer me and fit me for every fight. I guess this is going to be a big one, and you might stick up a prayer for us all, dear. I think someone will listen to you, Jess, because of our love and your big heart.

I've told you everything, but don't give it all to your folk. Of course I leave it all in your hands, but perhaps you might just talk about threatened pneumonia, till we can say more. In any case you needn't disguise how serious it is. That is too painfully evident. All my love, my own loyal darling.

Your boy

9 Mansion House Drive

18th July 1913

My darling

I hope you will get this on Saturday, but if you don't please forgive me. I had to go right into town after breakfast and I only got out half an hour ago - 5.30 p.m. Last night I had to hunt up Allan to perform a marriage at 8 o'clock this morning. The guv'nor had been kind of delirious all day and only remembered about midnight. I had a good deal of trouble to get a man for Sunday, but I got one at last. So that is one worry less. Dad is a little better to-day and Davidson finds his chest a good bit clearer. I hope that the pneumonia danger is passing over. His heart is quite good, but that is the chief danger now, as his temperature is still pretty high, and the fever is a big strain on a weakened heart. I didn't announce myself to him yesterday as it might have upset him, and when I went in to-day, the poor old chap broke down completely, and I myself played the fool a bit. It's only at times like that that one recognises how dearly one loves one's folk. Let me mix gay with grave. I had lunch in Craig's - and one of the little waitresses conquered by my sorrowful *beaux yeux* made me an offering of sweet peas. I hasten to lay the captives of my bow and spear at the feet of the only little woman. Wear them for our love. I'm not going to say how I felt and feel about leaving you because you know your own feelings. My dearest love to you, sweetheart.

Your own boy,

Hugh

9 Mansion House Drive
19th July 1913

Dear Jess

Just a tick to let you know how things are. Thank Heaven it's not so bad as it looked at first. Temperature is away down to 98^0 and respiration is likewise more normal. He didn't sleep at all last night, but in spite of that he looks more himself this morning. The doctor hasn't been in this morning but nurse thinks it has been acute gastritis due possibly to food poisoning, or something like that. I'm in a desperate hurry - due in Dumbarton to-night and I can safely go, so we all feel cheerier to-day. Thanks dear, for your love - I don't quite fix where I would be without it - you have all mine, my bonnie sweetheart.

Yours always,

Hugh

Sunday night 12 o'clock

Dear Jess

This is too terrible to write. I was having supper in Dumbarton when Tim rang up for me to come home at once. I got in here after walking from Parkhead about half an hour ago. Father was seized with severe pain at 3 last night and he has been dangerously ill ever since. He is under morphia just now and his groans and cries are heart-rending. Davidson got Middleton out this afternoon and he examined him thoroughly. He said that the illness was very obscure, that it wasn't pneumonia but that it might be pleurisy very deep seated. In any case he was acutely ill. He suggested a surgeon, and Paterson came out. He too overhauled him and there was a long consultation. Paterson doesn't know what it is either except possibly pleurisy or a form of appendicitis. He too told us frankly about the danger father is in. He is coming out to-morrow morning to see if there is any chance of operating. It can't go on long like this, for he has had no sleep for three days, and his eyes are sunken into his head. He is terribly worn. Mother is in a fearful state: won't leave his bedside, tho' there are two nurses now, and Tim I have sent off to bed utterly worn out. It is very bad for him; but what can we do. I am sitting waiting for my aunt, the doctor, who is motoring through from Edinburgh. What a Sunday night and what a journey that was. It will nightmare me for many a day. Oh Jess, I don't know what's going to happen and I'm afraid to think. If you just heard my dear dad's cries. God help us all.

10 a.m. Monday

In a rush. Thanks for your note. I'll see Dada[10] to-day if I can. My dad is much about the same. Auntie Kate and Davidson diagnose pleuro-pneumonia - very deep at the base of the right lung.

All my love, dearest

> 9 Mansion House Drive
>
> 22nd July 1913

Dear Jess

This is a very hurried scrawl. I have been on my feet most of the night, and there are many things to do. Affairs are very critical with father. His weakness is great and it is continually increasing. There must be a crisis soon or he cannot hold out longer. His heart is getting very feeble and they had to give strychnine twice last night. I found a half hour to see your Dada yesterday. He is quite cheery and comfortable, tho' he is cut up about my guv'nor. Jess, it can't be much worse, and I am terrified lest mother should break down. She is very overwrought. My dear love to you, sweetheart *ex profundis.*

Yours,

Hugh

There was no letter from you this morning.

> 9 Mansion House Drive
>
> 22nd July 1913

Dearest Jess

I'm beginning this letter to you at 7 o'clock on Tuesday night and I don't know how it will finish. There is less running about for me to do, and my only resource is to speak to you, because you understand so well.

Dr. Davidson says it is not utterly hopeless yet, but Auntie Kate is in great anxiety. The heart has quickened enormously and it is also intermittent. I felt his pulse to-night and it goes in spurts with long pauses. They are giving thirty grains of strychnine every four hours now, also digitalis and brandy. I'm afraid to think of the night. It will go hard with him.

It seems days since this morning, and I can't remember whether I told you of my midnight prowl last night. I had a hunt for some stuff from 9 till 1.30 - but I got it in the end. I had to arouse Watson the Chemist from his slumbers. I had three hours of sleep last night on a sofa, but I am in for an all-night-up business to-night, I fear.

I saw your dada for a little this afternoon. I was glad to go if only to discipline oneself against a selfish point of view about one's own particular worries. He is much cheerier and better in every way; but I fear my visits only depress him with the sad news I carry. Jess dear, there has been an extra worry at the back of my head all day. Are you not well that you didn't write? If you just missed it by accident, please dear don't be angry with me for bothering you about it. But my nerves are so jangled that I imagine all kinds of things and it's rather torturesome. I've seen the quick change from health and love and life to the doorstep of Beyond so often now that I'm getting cowardly where you are concerned. Oh my dear, don't be angry. I'm just babbling on. You see I've to look happy before mother and the rest, and I'm all slack and out now.

12 midnight

Jess, I am sitting up in the study. Auntie Kate won't leave father for a moment, and we persuaded mother to take my room downstairs and leave me within call. They say to-night will make a difference - which means____. Jess, I have had hours of waiting, and I have read over all your letters to me right from the beginning - the first one dates from July 1911. Some day you and I will read them over together before our own fireside - then you will realise how much you have been to your laddie. There has been no letter where you missed out to say how you loved me. Dear, I cried over some of them. I am soft and all unstrung just now, and my love to you first cried out for the nearness of you. Your love and your sympathy are great things just now - but, oh Jess for your presence, dearest one. I'm going to try for some sleep as I am getting played out.

4.30

Dear I got from 2 o'clock till just now, and I am much refreshed. Dad is holding on, and I'm praying that his heart will steady up. I have just been sitting with him for an hour or so. He likes to have one of us near him, and Auntie Kate had to lie down - poor soul, she is worn out. Dad can't get much sleep and he is in great discomfort. He asked me if I thought he was going to die. It fairly got me, but I managed to carry it off without frightening him. He thinks he has only got pleurisy, but he knows he is desperately ill. Dear, I hope you will never see any one you love like this. It is very sore listening to that kind of breathing, and to know any moment may be the last. I've wished so often I could give dada my heart to carry him over the crisis. I hope you won't have to experience it, Jess, but I am a good nurse for a man. Several times I have put him to sleep just by holding his hand and sitting quiet. It's quite bright outside, another fine day - the anxiety is what tells on one. I do hope mother has slept for she needed it terribly last night. Tim is sleeping up at the Truant School these nights. He is very anxious to stand in, but we daren't let him do much. The Thomsons are very kind. They can't do enough for us.

He has lived the night and Dr says 'more hopeful'.

9 Mansion House Drive

23rd July 1913

Dearest Jess

It is just after ten o'clock and I have been thinking long about you. I had a very kind note from Alison to-night, thank her for it. This has been a bad day for us. In the morning we were all hopeful. Father's pulse was quieter and more regular. He continued so till the afternoon and then he developed a severe pain in his left side - the pneumonia has gone into his other lung, and that means double work on his already overburdened heart. Can you see any escape? - I can't.

Mother is in a terrible state. She is certain that it is the beginning of the end. I shall be up again to-night. It is too dangerous to take my clothes off. Poor Tim went away to-night crying. He is afraid he will not see him again. I saw your dada again this afternoon. Your uncle from Edinburgh was there. I like him. I told dada the good news and said I would see him to-morrow. I wonder if I will? I'll send you a wire if anything happens, which God forbid.

My love, if you knew how I'm thinking of you, and leaning on you, I fancy you would be glad. If you were here with your strong little body, how you would help mother! Jess, Jess.

Good-night,

Hugh

9 Mansion House Drive

24th July 1913

Darling

I have your dear letter this morning. I can't tell you how close you come to me. In these long nights I often really feel you in my arms, and I can hear you talking to me. Dear one, things are black. My dear dad has the smallest chance. He is not suffering pain now, and we bless God for that. Up till to-day he has been in acute misery. His heart is beating and nothing more this morning. Dear, I can hardly write to-day. But I must go on and do all I can for our household. You won't mind if I don't write more - my dearest love - I hold you fast. Oh Jess, Jess! This is terrible.

Hugh

My poor mother -

9 Mansion House Drive

25th July 1913

My dear one

Father is still living, but he is very weak. Poor mother is in a constant half-break down, and she is feeling the strain most dreadfully. I was sent off to bed last night, and got my clothes off for the first time for three nights. I slept like a log, for mother had tried to rouse me about 12 and she hadn't managed it. Dad's heart is flagging, Jess, and there is danger in every moment. His mind is quite clear, and he is realising his state. He broke us all down last night by talking of things. I hope I have as good a record when I am where he is to-day. It is -

Jess, the doctor has just been in and he says dad is better a bit to-day. Dear, isn't it great. There's a chance yet. My dear I want him to know you, and I want you to love him some day as I do - and please God we shall have that joy yet.

I see the bursary list is out. I am sorry for your sake and because of your hard work over it, but for no other reason. You had too much to do at one time. My love, I am so happy just now, I can almost see my dear dad on his feet again. I hope it may not be false optimism.

Your husband

9 Mansion House Drive

11.30 p.m. 25th July 1913

Dear

I am going to have another night's vigil. I sent mother off to bed, and I am a cinch for the study sofa. I am to be pulled up at 2 that Auntie Kate may get some rest, and the other nurse and I will watch till the morning. This morning's hope was a bit rosy. One suffers from reaction even in the matter of expression. Dad has passed a comfortable day, but to-night his pulse is intermitting again. This is very bad. But we are just trusting on, Jess, and working our hardest. I am feeling a wee bit relieved about my own work to-night. I was rather dreading the three services on Sunday, but Uncle Jimmy has offered to take all mine if I take his two in Barrhead. This helps a lot.

What am I to say to you, dear, about your two letters to-day? Two, Jess! I just sat and looked at the envelope of the one that came in to-night. And, dear, no one but you could have written it. I think from what you say that you are guessing what they mean to me just now. They are just like direct answers to prayer. They keep me going like daily bread. My love, I look to you every hour of the day. When I am dead tired and there are heaps of messages to do, my thoughts fly to your dear heart and I forget that I am tired. My little wife, how you will be welcomed into our home circle. You shall see what a house-furnisher true love is. I love that hackneyed phrase 'true love'. The old poets never did without it - you are my true love and I am yours. Dear, I am glad you are praying for my dad. I don't think God himself could say 'No' to my little Jess. I don't mean that either for false humour nor for blasphemy. Dear, I kiss your red lips, and I draw you to me. I can feel your body under my arm and your head on my shoulder. Dear, I'm always brave then. I'll turn in; it's getting late. My last thoughts are with you.

Morning

Dear. I was sent up for Tim at 6 o'clock. Auntie Kate says father is getting weaker, and both his pulse and his respiration are very bad. I fear this comes to an end. I have your letter, my dear love. I know how you want to be here - no more than I want you. But we just have to stick it out. Jess, I begin to think life is just one long policy of 'stick it out'. I've been doing nothing else for days. God keep you, my lass,

Your boy

Telegram   28th July 1913

Post Office Telegraphs

Glasgow

To: Reid, Thundergay, Pirnmill

Father died yesterday morning at 12.45

Hugh

Chapter 5

"And so you are not to know him. I am sorry because he would have guided us through many deep waters, and he would have rejoiced in our love."

Hugh's father, the Rev J Wallace Mann, minister of Eastbank United Free Church in Shettleston, died on the 27 July at the age of fifty-three. Originally from Nairn, he was educated at the Royal High School in Edinburgh and at Edinburgh University. His early ministry was at Langholm in Dumfriesshire where Hugh was born. During his twelve years in Shettleston he was responsible for a new church being built for the Eastbank United Free Church to accommodate a congregation which had increased under his stewardship from one hundred and seventy-six to six hundred. An obituary states that "Mr Mann soon drew around him a large band of zealous supporters, and to-day the various organisations connected with the church are in a vigorous condition. One phase of Mr. Mann's activities which greatly endeared him to the congregation was his work on behalf of the young. He added to genuine sympathy as a pastor a quiet charm of manner which appealed to young and old alike. His loss will be deeply felt, not only by the members of the congregation but by all his ministerial colleagues in Glasgow, in whose presbyterial deliberations he was recognised as a sagacious and kindly counsellor. He is survived by a widow and two sons."

The United Free Church of Scotland is a Presbyterian church formed in 1900 as a result of the union between the Free Church of Scotland and the United Presbyterian Church. In 1910 the World Missionary Conference was held in the General Assembly Hall of the United Free Church in Edinburgh. This Conference has come to be regarded as the first milestone in the Protestant Ecumenical Movement. In 1929, with the exception of a small minority of congregations which are still active today, the United Free Church united with the Church of Scotland.

All Hugh's letters for the next year are written on black-edged bereavement paper.

9 Mansion House Drive
Shettleston
29th July 1913

Dear Jess

And so you are not to know him. I am sorry, because he would have guided us through many deep waters, and he would have rejoiced in our love. Your father will be sore at not getting up for my daddy's funeral. We are burying him just facing his friend Hector, and I think he will be pleased. Dear, I can't write any more. I am the sorrowful head of our house, and there is much to do.

Yours always,

Hugh

7.30 p.m.

Dear little woman

Mother has not come in yet. I am afraid she will be very tired when she does transpire. This is just to tell you what a fine lass you are. I am glad you are strong - for you are, you know. I am thinking that there must be some latent quality of good in me if I have drawn out your love to me. One can't be an absolute rotter and win the love of a good woman, can one? I wish I could find words to tell you how proud you have made me by the gift of your love. I have just three big ambitions in my life. One is to preach the Gospel of Jesus like a true man, fearlessly. The second is to make mother happy. The other; and I hardly dare say it is the dearest, tho' one ought not, is to make your life with me to which we both look forward so much, a happy one. I want you not so much to have a surface happy life, as a life where the joy is a deep undercurrent to sweeten your whole life. It's a difficult thing to do, to keep things sweet amid petty annoyances and great sorrows which must come to us, but it's a great thing to do, and I can be satisfied with nothing less. I'm not going to make any rash promises, but if a man can shield a woman by his love, you shall be guarded well when you come to me. I've often wondered in my unregenerate and easy-loving days, how the great love of my life would take me. And I find that tho' it has left me a lot of boyish tricks, it has deepened tremendously my sense of responsibility, and it has filled me with some new spirit - almost, if one weren't afraid of the word - a consecration. I like to think of our love as a thing as strong as the oak's roots, and yet as beautiful as the summer's rose. I think it is - mostly from the way folk treat us. People are always glad of a beautiful thing, and they are very indulgent to it. So are they to us - very kind - and even if they do smile - it is a very tender sort of smile.

      Jess, I come back to the point to say you are very brave. Dear, I'm glad; it will make many of the things we have got to pass thro' less black, less soul-destroying, easier to be borne. I'm jumping a long way ahead I know, but it's always worth while reckoning out what lies ahead, and I think I see a gleam, as of a silver shore. You and I, dearest, are going to be a very happy lad and lass, and though the life we shall lead may seem a quiet one to outsiders, I don't think we shall be fatigued by it.

My dear, if I could only speak to you now; sometimes I can, other times I just want to look at you, and to love you. Darling, I kiss you good-night.

Your boy,

Hugh

I like to hear you say 'Hugh'; it sounds prettier on your lips then on any other: you manage to get such a dear possessive ring into it. Don't answer, this is just a rhapsody.

16 Drummond Place

Edinburgh

5th August 1913

Dear

As you would guess, we did not get away till this morning. I saw your green jersey wending homeward as the ten o'clock Edinburgh left Shettleston, and I was muchly wishing you had been ten minutes earlier. We got thro' quite snugly, and I have been loafing around in the cultured air of Drummond Place Gardens most of the afternoon. There has been a lot of trouble fixing a place wherein to rest the soles of our feet. I wired to Arisaig this evening, and we are waiting for the reply. Well, Jess, you and I are having our ups and downs, and just at present it's mostly 'downs', but we have put our heads together - most literally upon occasion, and I guess the 'ups' are on the next mail. What does it matter even if they are long overdue, so long as you plus me equals us - I'm no shakes at maths but that equation seems to be a simple one. I'm in demand here, and I must rip off.

All my love, dearest,

Your boy

16 Drummond Place

Edinburgh

7th August 1913

My darling Jess

I have your letter - also your very flattering engravure of your pretty features. It's 'not *bed*'.

We are still here, but we leave to-morrow for a weird address - Culreoch, Kilchrenan, Loch Awe. Don't send anything there till I write you from it, because we have done everything by telegram, and for all we know about it, it may be the *rankest* flea-run in Scotland. We're hoping not, but *l'homme propose, et Dieu dispose* or words to that effect. The cultured air of Edinburgh gets a little on my nerves. I was out golfing last night with my uncle on one of the blue-blood courses - Edinburgh Burgess - and I found what an effort is necessary to look like the tag end of a ducal line.

Dear lass, what a loving little thing it is, and it thinks we are quite an ordinary couple, does it, and that parting is a sweet sorrow to quote my old friend Bill. Does she so soon forget?

Well, well, you may call us any name you like so long as you don't separate us from our love. I'm to be busy again to-day.

All my love, dearest.

Hugh

Chapter 6

"The worst of any holiday is the distance it takes me from the centre of things. Do you recognise yourself under that new name?"

Following the death of his father Hugh and his family spend some time near Loch Awe in the west of Scotland. They travelled by train to Oban on a line skirting the top of the long, narrow loch which begins near the foot of Ben Cruachan and stretches about twenty-five miles to the south-west.

Culreoch, Kilchrenan, circa 1935

Culreoch

Kilchrenan

Loch Awe

Saturday

Ownest Angel

In the nature of the case I haven't heard from you for two days, and I ain't goin' to for two more - maybe three - and so I'm wanting the touch of you extra bad. The worst of any holiday is the distance it takes me from the centre of things. Do you recognise yourself under that new name? We had the gravest qualms about this place. To begin with they only wanted £7 for the house till the end of the month and the attraction included four bedrooms, two sitting rooms, bathroom, stables, pony and trap, garden produce, free fishing on Loch Awe and a private boat - oh and I forgot - a mangle. We couldn't understand how it was to be done at the price. But here we are in a fine farm-house with everything better than we could expect -

for the place is scrupulously clean, and there is a glorious view of the loch and of Ben Cruachan. You will be ready by this time for the next remark, which is that this is the very spot for our honeymoon. There are remarkably few people about - indeed a human being is an event to be eagerly discussed. Could anything be more blessed, you little darling! Also there is an improvement on Arran in the important matter of sanitation which is modern and perfect. You will gather that we are in clover.

Let me tell you how we got here. First of all we had luggage which constituted a regular flitting - I had 8/8 excess to pay. We came up the Oban line, through Callander, Crianlarich, and Dalmally to Loch Awe Station at the head of the loch. The scenery was absolutely clinking, Ben Ledi, Ben Vorlich, Ben More, Ben Cruachan, and I met Ben Wilson on the pier. We embarked upon the stately screw steamer 'Caledonia' - 20 feet by 7 - called so I fancy because the skipper was 'stern and wild' - he certainly was if one may judge from his language when the crew - a nice-looking lad - dropped our provision box on his corns. After an hour's drifting - they called it steaming I believe - but little steamed save the kettle for the skipper's cup of tea - we got alongside two paling slabs and a plank across - locally known as Taycreggan Pier. Ten minutes driving through picturesque scenery brought us to our palatial abode (consult any guide-book).

Here I am this morning in the old grey flannel breeks and those dinky brown shoes - last worn you know where. I have also on my aged coat in the button-hole of which are two withered stems - but the flower that once was growing is forget-me-not, and I haven't - either the flower or who gave it. My dear, dear Jess, I'm just loving you. You'll be nearly alone now. Think of me often often as I think of you ditto ditto.

All my love darlingest wife,

Your husband

Culreoch

Kilchrenan

Loch Awe

11th August 1913

My dear

I have been rather lazy this morning, and behold at 11.30 I am just enclothed. It is a most excellent day, and the loch is glittering like some far-flung star. Observe how the environment is affecting my usually irreproachable diction. I've been thinking of you a lot, which probably accounts for an extra bad dream I had last night, wherein damnable hands pulled you away from me. You cried out to me to hold you, but I couldn't, and you disappeared, and I never saw you again. No wonder I have a beastly headache this morning. Little girl, I took my aunt an arm-walk in the late dusk last night. The stars were out in millions upon millions. And we walked over the hill and stood looking down the loch - seeing twenty miles of water and wood and hill and over all the darkness of glen and mountain - and I bethought me in a sadness of your absence from my side, where I would fain have held you everlastingly. Kid, Kid. Do you know how the Campbells left their hills to follow Charlie in the '45, and how when Culloden had been lost one Campbell said to another, 'It's a far cry to Loch Awe'. I feel that it's a far cry from Loch Awe to my city of dreams beyond the rim of the sky.

Amn't I shooting out my melancholy neck to a pathetic extent? Never heed, I'll stop now and descend to practicalities. And right here I have a confession. I played the heathen *yestre'en*, and went not nigh the house of God. What sayest thou to that, stern ruler of my destiny? Excuse follows - to wit that the only service was at 6 o'clock in the evening, that the beauty of the night defied me to enclose my person in a poky little schoolroom for the purpose of *hearkening* unto a diminutive individual with bandy legs holding forth on such a mystical theme as 'The Wells of Salvation'. I believe they were (1) Well! (2) Well! (3) Well!!!

Am I pardoned, my bonnie *li'l* Kiddie? I think I am a trifle mad this morning. Use that key to unlock the riddles of this ridiculous letter. But despite all solecisms and anachronisms, to which latter class I have an idea I myself belong, believe me to be

Ever your true lover

Culreoch

Kilchrenan

12th August 1913

Dearest Jess

I haven't heard from you yet in this forsaken spot. If my father had lived, he would have been fifty-four to-day. We are thinking back over the jolly twelfths we have had. We used to chaff him what a pity it was he wasn't a pheasant, so that he might have been shot on his birthday. Quite recently when he was ill, he told the doctor that he would be fifty-four in a fortnight if he were spared. After an experience such as we have had little things become prophetic.

We are lazing away the days, though I am getting a bit of work in too. Beautiful weather, warm days. I'm thinking of sleeping out under the trees away up on the hill-side. There is too little air in the house, and I find it difficult to get to sleep. I lay long last night, and all my thought was how I loved you. I tried to stand back and analyse. But I didn't get very far. I lost myself in watching to catch your figure and hold you in my arms. Jess, I can ill do wanting you. I'm doing my best here to keep things bright, but *quis custodiet ipsos custodes*. All my love, dear one.

Yours always,

Hugh

Culreoch

Kilchrenan

Monday morning

Sweetheart

I begin to pity you. I fear you have fixed upon an imbecile as your husband that is to be. The reason annexed to the above doctrine is *cela*. Last night my aunt and I spent under the vault of heaven or the canopy of the sky - take either slushy epithet you like. We went away up the hill and slung our hammock between two trees. The aunt entered and was duly wrapped up. Then I got the extension deck chair - a *d - d* uncomfortable couch. Our idea was that the fine air would make us sleep sound. Is it necessary to mention the fact that we did not sleep at all? We lay chattering till about one and then the heather moon was high with a reflection like the gates of the New Jerusalem on the Loch, and the stars were as usual, starry, only more so. The trees were talking and the little creepy crawlies were creepy-crawlying. Naturally we did not sleep. But it was a glorious experience. It got beastly cold between two and four, and the sun rose over the eastern Cruachan range, and things were too blinkin' bonnie to sleep. We had a little spirit lamp and I brewed a dinky cup of tea and we were jolly happy. A spider popped out of my shoe, which I had taken off; and a wasp settled on my face, and remained as I thought an age, while I hardly dared to breathe, but these were the minor worries.

Well, what do you think of your mad youth? We'll maybe do that kind of thing together some time. It is rather fine. One thinks a lot with the whole world spread out before one, and no one awake to claim it. I thought much of a little girl lying asleep such a long way off and I rather loved that sleepy little girl - ah! Now you ask. And now the boy was – Me.

Culreoch

Kilchrenan

Wednesday

Dearest Jess

I've waited for the post this morning and your dear letter has just come in. Poor wee darling, I'm on to your loneliness, for I'm suffering from the same worry. In this ends-of-the-earth hole there's nothing to do but reflect on happier days. Don't cry, though little one, because I'm not there to kiss the tears away and give you exactly what you want at the moment.

I got your snapshot *yestre'en*. I've been kissing in stealthily at intervals since. I'm going to send you this other of Brodick. You've seen it before, but it's all I have. Keep it and bring it to our home when we marry, for I don't want to lose sight of these other fellows.

There is a sale of work in the church of the bandy-legged parson to-day. I've met his wife - a cultured Glasgow woman. Mother remarked to me that there must be a very strong bond of love when a woman will give up career and prospects to share a humble country manse. I said, "So there is". Rather put my foot in it, didn't I?

I'm sure certain you'll manage the youngsters, old girl. If you don't, it will be their fault, and you'll just hand them over to their daddy for suitable correction. That reminds me that the furnishing of our manse must include good leather slippers. Cheer up, old darling, I'll be home on Thursday week, if I can get away, and it will be dash funny if I can't get up that night. I finish, my darling Jess, by handing over to you all the love of my being.

Your own lad

Culreoch

Kilchrenan

14th August 1913

I'm a bully, am I? And I won't get the photo? My lassie, just you wait till I can bring *force majeure* to bear upon you, and then we shall see who is as it were what! You little darling, do you think I'm going to waste time being jealous over the irresponsible 5 feet NOTHING sweet seventeen? My good child, you flatter yourself? I hear you grind your teeth and swear to bring me to your knees and my senses. Never heed. I've done the knees bit already, and the other is hopeless for I ain't got none.

Yesterday I walked seven miles to Taynuilt thro' Glen Nant - stunning country. Then took train thro' the Pass of Brander to Loch Awe Station and two shillings worth of "Caledonia" - the wet nurse for a poetic child'back to Taycreggan. Nice round.

I've been very busy with cards of acknowledgement. So far I've done two hundred of them and I'm not nearly finished. There was a sale of work at the U.F. church yesterday which I honoured at night. They made £50, 3/9 of which was mine. This breaks all records for the neighbourhood. You think you won't scorch my shirts? I never heard of any one doing that, but if it is a new and original method of maltreating linen, may the Lord have mercy on your soul if you venture to experiment on me. All my love, dear heart.

Yours ever,

Hugh

Je t'embrasse. Till ten to-night.

Culreoch

Kilchrenan

15th August 1913

Dearest Jess

Like my dear friend Miss A. Laurie, your voice is low and sweet, and you're a' the world tae me, but you have not written to me to-day. This is very deplorable in one whose neck is like the swan. If you don't write regularly you can't expect me to lay me down an' die for you, now can you? Be reasonable! I always get down in the mouth when I don't hear from you, and as you know the cavernous quality of the aforesaid mouth, I regard it as a refinement of cruelty to permit me to get down in it. *Regardez-vous igitur, m'selle.*

The weather has burst its braces. Yesterday it Scotch misted and to-day it is Scotch hopelessly lost. It has taken the wrong turning at the girl's cross-roads. If it doesn't pick up soon, I shall pick up my bags (no reference to clothing) and come home.

We went out in our boat yesterday. It is twice the weight of the Pirnmill ferry and I had a stiff job pulling it. I conveyed my mother and my two aunts well into the middle of the loch, when we found the water coming thro' a crack like a water-tap. Then it was pull for the shore, sailor. We got in with the boat half-full of Loch Awe and all we could do was to stand arms akimbo, and wail 'Awe.' You dearest little darling, I wish I had you here to cuddle - a plebeian word - perhaps one should say embrace. Would you snuggle up to me? You might have written any way - swine - *cochin - vous êtes, n'est ce-pas?* Ten thousand kisses, little one.

Your own neglected Laddie

Culreoch

Kilchrenan

16th August 1913

You Jess

If I hadn't got your letter this morning I was sending a wire, so you know what you risk when you don't write. The wording would have run like this. "Anything wrong, darling? Your Hugh". How would you have liked facing Shettleston Post Office after that? I'm not looking solemn in that photo, simply self-contained and dignified, and as for the moustache one, its history will make you jealous so you won't hear it till I can kiss you better on the spot. Did you ever have your lips called a spot before?

You talk about a year making a difference in one's life. Why yes, doesn't it? Observe how my character has changed for the worse since you chained me up. I am now a mere degenerate instead of the erstwhile young Apollo. Now, don't you start a-smilin'. I have heard a lovely Highland song which I must get when I come home. Jess, I am fearfully fed up here. I'm only sticking it out because of the mater, otherwise I would have been home ruining your Jugurtha business long ago. The weather has simply gone to Hades. It is rainy, and misty and stuffy and - - y (of centuries fame). One can do nothing but sit and curse because of it. And this latter I am attacking in the fine spirit of the Johnny who wrote, "To do but one thing all the day, and do that one thing well." All my love, sweetest wee soul.

Ever your lover,

Hugh

Culreoch

Kilchrenan

19th August 1913

Darling

Last note for another spell. I managed your French all right, you cheeky young thing. I'm home on Thursday, and if the train is on time I'll be out on the 3.24 to Shettleston. If you are a Christian you will fake a message into town and come out on that train, particularly as I won't see you that night - you and your party.

If you think I am coming up the hill to loaf and be merry, I now disillusion you. I've the very deuce and all work to do. You must help me - of course all work and no philandering makes Hugh a silly pig, and we must avoid that.

I'm in a great hurry to-day, and thundering happy so *cela finit mes remarques!*

Thine,

Hugonem W. M

Love to Aunt Mary.

Your letter just in. DAMN the Thundergay gathering, the Rosses and everything and body that keeps you from me.

Culreoch before and after restoration, 1990 and 1998

Chapter 7

"You and I are 'us' without a doubt, and no passing of years can change that in this or in any other world."

While still engaged in his work as a Student Missionary at Wellpark Church, Hugh prepares for his examinations at the United Free Church College. Following the next letter, written in September, there is silence, presumably because Hugh and Jessie are in regular contact. Jessie, now eighteen, follows in Hugh's footsteps to the Faculty of Arts at The University of Glasgow to study Latin and Mathematics in her first year. In December Hugh visits his brother Tim, who, for the good of his health has been advised to take up farming, and is now a trainee farmer on a farm in Midlothian. Following Hugh's father's death Hugh's mother moves to Edinburgh and in January Hugh takes up residency in North Kelvinside near Glasgow's Great Western Road.

9 Mansion House Drive

Saturday afternoon

Dearest Jess

It is a grey day, and my soul is also grey. I weary for you. My aunt came up from Ayr this morning and she remains till Monday. I have been working steadily since you left me. I wrote a sermon last night, a thundering bad one. I had no heart for it, but it had to be done. I sometimes think life is kind of hard to us, but this may be a snare and a delusion. Anyhow it will come right one day.

Exams thus -

Wed 1st Oct   10-12 Scrip. Kn; 3.30-5.30 N.T. Pt 1

Thurs 2nd Oct   10-12 N.T. Pt 11; 3.30-5.50 O.T. Pt 1

Fri 3rd Oct   10-12 O.T Pt 11; 12.15-2.15 Apologetics; 2.30-3.30 Presbytery; 3.30-5.50 Junior Systematic!!!

That's a cheery lot. I may get up on Friday evening, if I still exist. Please have that text 'Praise ye the Lord' ready for Friday evening. I'm just going to Barrhead - thorns and maledictions upon it.

All my love

Monday - confounded-day. Afternoon

Etiam survivo, mirabile dictu! I had a racketty day on Sunday. There are five youngsters at my uncle's manse - eldest nine, youngest 18 months and if one isn't yelling, it's because two are. I live thro' a gay time, and gained everlasting popularity because I let them crawl over my best coat. They are all more or less moulting and I had to be brushed frequently. I was done up when I got into Wellpark, and my prayer-meeting came into the vestry at 6.30 and found me asleep on the sofa. It was very undignified, but highly amusing. I hope you've had a good time at Dumfries. This ticket came this morning in an advertisement. I can't use it, but some of your folks may be able to. I suspect you will be shown round the premises with it and also pressed to purchase shares. However if you care to risk that, you may use it with my blessing. I must now resume the thrilling task of exegeting Paul to the Colossians. My dearest love to you, sweetheart.

Yours ever,

Hugh

Remote

Ford

Midlothian

31st December 1913

Dearest Jess

I was tremendously and gloriously surprised to get your dutiful wifely letter this morning - (Drat this pen!). This is the first time you have written before I have, and I am charmed to believe that your sense of responsibility is increasing. How did the dinner taste? I am sure it was not so nice as my letter.

Tim has gone off to Edinburgh this morning but there is a youngster of fourteen here for his holiday, and as he has divided his hero-worship between us, it becomes painfully concentrated when Tim is away. Result, no peace. I'm having a very quiet decent time here. There has been snow since I came, and we spent yesterday sledging. I hadn't sledged for years - the old man speaks. And so you think I need someone to look after me! Do you know I refused an invitation with Tim to a party to-night: I can't be bothered glad-eying girls when you are not around.

You'll get this letter on New Year morning, and so a very good and glad one to you, my dear. But we will have better ones yet. I remember a letter I got from you this time last year, and you were in the dumps because it was so long to look ahead. Sweetheart, it's a year nearer now; and before we know where we are it will have come right. You and I are 'us' beyond a doubt, and no passing of years can change that in this or in any other world. *Omnia vincit amor, et nos cedamus amori!* You see I haven't forgotten all my Latin. Dash that kid; he's howling for me to come and sledge. I'm being butchered to make a Remote holiday. I send you all my love, darling.

Ever your boy,

Hugh

Remote

Ford

4th January 1914

Dear

Thanks for your letter. This is to be a disappointing little scribble. Don't send any more letters here, as I am leaving on Tuesday. Tim is going in to Edinburgh for a month's classes and I shall just go with him so I shall not have any fixed address or abode for two or three days. I rather fancy I shall go home on Wednesday, in which case I may get out before the meeting on Thursday night, but only if my address is finished.

This is Tim's birthday. He is twenty. So we are all getting out of the 'teens. But poor wee 'you' must linger there awhile yet. But 'there, little girl, don't cry.' You and I love; *ergo quid* plus *voulez-vous?*

See you soon,

Il Bacchanale

5 Wilton Mansions

N Kelvinside

Saturday evening

Dearest

I found this as I was reading Henley to-night. He must have thought our way once.

'A wink from Hesper falling
Fast in the wintry sky
Comes through the even blue
Dear, like a word from you.
Is it good-bye?

Across the miles between us
I send you sign for sign
Good-night, sweet heart, good-night:
Till life and all take flight,
Never good-bye.'

I love you so utterly, Jess, and I am very lonely without you, even though I have been very busy. Dear, I must see you soon, and I shall try to get out on Tuesday afternoon. I wonder if you will be in. You see I'm not certain that I will get out, but if you think it's worth risking, and if you are not busy otherwise, you might be about. My ownest little darling, I can feel you in my arms, and I see your face turned up to me for kisses. Jess, I kiss you, and on Tuesday *dabo milia basia* or thereabouts.

Jimmy Mackintosh has been helping me to arrange my books, which has been rather a mighty task. However we are nearly finished now, and may the Lord be praised. I'll give you all news when I see you. Pray that it be soon. We have had so many visitors to-day that it is now 9.30 and I have two-thirds of my sermon to write. You shall sleep while I watch the minute-hand creep round and work the while.

Good-night my dearest love,

Till life and all take flight,

Never good-bye.

Your own laddie,

Hugh

> 5 Wilton Mansions
> N Kelvinside
> 29th January 1914

Dearest

Extract from my (your) diary - February 2. Monday: 9.45 MacFadyen; 11.00 Music; 2.00 Play organ in St. Vincent St. U.F. Church for McQueen's Conference - 500 ministers or thereby; 4.00 Visit Granny Morrison who may be dead before then.

So you see there would be no time at all for us if I came out on that day. Unless I hear otherwise from you, I'll come out on Tuesday. I have a Workers' Social at night, but it must just take its chance. Anyway I love you. I'm just in from my meeting very fed up with a rotten cold. So *je vais à mon lit!* To your lovely eyes, my darling. I don't suppose you will get this until some time on Saturday, and as you may have a bad conscience then, and as you certainly will have a weary body, probably you will be angry with me; but don't like a dear, for I can't help it. You know I would much rather be out loving darling wee you. D - McQueen, D - Dennistoun, D - everything that keeps up apart.

All my love, Jess dear. Always and always,

Your boy

> 5 Wilton Mansions
> Kelvinside N
> Glasgow
> 15th March 1914

Dearest Jess

It groweth late upon the Sabbath night, and I will soon depart. I am in slightly gloomier mood than usual at the moment, and it is always then I seem to reach out most for you. There is a curious weak spot in a man's armour-plating, and the only thing that makes it strong is a weak woman. Quaint, isn't it? Human nature is one of the most amusing studies under heaven. I had a tiresome day yesterday, and my one decent time was at night when by no mere chance but by a merciful design of a merciful Providence I dreamt of you. It seems that, not content with cursing my waking hours, you propose to haunt my sleeping ones.

Dear, I hope you will have tremendously good luck in your exams. You know how I live in all that you do, and so too you know how golden my wishes are for you. I don't want anything poor or harsh to come into your life, and I'll do my best to fill the circle of your days with the things that are worth while. Till then I suppose we must just peg each other along with all the courage we can collect. Anyhow nothing can rob us of our city of desire.

It is a strange thing how I can compel your physical presence when I think long of you. Just now I can touch the curl of your hair, and catch the glorious looks you keep for me. My dear love, I haven't said at all what I mean, and I suppose I never shall, but I feel mightier somehow.

Yours,

Hugh

5 Wilton Mansions

22nd April 1914

Dearest lassie

Sorry I can't turn up. I guess you know how I have to parcel out my time these strenuous days, and an extra call leaves Percy gasping. Sorry a thousand times. You have nothing to apologise for, you silly wee darling. You were fed up, that's all. I had a note from Hector asking me to meet him Thursday or Friday. I wrote back saying that I was going to an ordination on Thursday and on Friday I had a most important engagement with his sister-in-law. I will be mighty near you this afternoon and yet mighty far. Golf with Jimmy McIntosh. He came in last night and rolled me into it while I was still protesting. Can I get kissing you sweetheart?... Thanks, wee one, that will carry me on fine for a bit.

Your boy

Friday 4.30

Oh, Jess darling, I'm sorry. I had a golf match on this morning, and I left at 9.45. I didn't get home till ten minutes ago. Isn't it ghastly? Have you gone down with the 4.18? I could kick myself round Arran. I do hope your toothache is better, dearest. What a time you must have had. I'm too sick to write any more, lass.

Your boy

8 Drumpark
Largo (not by Handel)
1st June 1914

My ownest lass

Picture your distracted lover in a jolly cold bed with a few piffling rags to cover him, endeavouring to raise the temperature by means of a flat-iron heated on a gas ring and swaddled in flannel. A most unromantic picture I admit, but these east coast winds are most searching. They have brought back traces of the gout I got in the mutiny in India in '57 in - oh Lord! There's too much 'in' about this. You will suspect that I have been consuming cider. Pardon my lightheadness, old one, but (1) I am on holiday, (2) I am very tired, (3) I am writing to you, my maddening little sweetheart, and I have just caught sight of your eyes. So I am only now beginning to recover my breath! We have not been able to discover where the confounded ass of a woman who owns this place keeps her hot-water bottles, and you have been warned what a cold .. I are - hence the flat-iron. Jane's brilliant suggestion.

We had a fairly rotten journey - frightfully slow. The train stood so long at that bally old Thornton Junction that it had to be dug out. I hope it is up to time next Saturday. We are to call in at Mrs Jarvie's on our way out, so that on Sunday afternoon she can take you straight up from Kirk. That will avoid any trouble or awkwardness should the Wilsons be there.

This is expensive paper, so I'm going to write on both sides thereof. This house is a great institution. It is in a little row, and it's the devil's job to know one's own house. It couldn't be nearer the sea unless it was in it. The full tide smites a breakwater six paces from our front doorstep. I do love to get close down to the sea like this, and to fall asleep with its bonnie chatter in my ears. Do you remember about the last night of the great Pirnmill week that we went down very, very close to the water's edge and talked in each other's arms of all that the future was to bring us. I can't recall much of what we said now, but I have a memory of my two loves talking to me together, and when you didn't interrupt the sea, and when the sea blended with you, I knew it was all right. And I loved you both the more. I'm as egotistical as ever, my dear. I can't seem to make it sufficiently clear to you that I am woefully, desperately, fatally in love. I haven't even the faint consolation that I may change. In my heart I see my doom written, for behold! Never can I cease to love you. Jess dear, I get kind of crazy when I reflect that you have promised to be my wife. Think of all that it means, my own darling. I break off, for it is just ten o' clock, and I am making my devotions to the biggest part of myself. Jess, my love, good-night.

Your husband!!! Great that, isn't it? Tell me about Latin, will you dear? I haven't been a bit anxious after Saturday.

Thursday morning 10.30

Dearest

You are in the thick of it just now, and I am trying to write a sermon without much success, for to speak truth my thoughts are with a wee lassie puzzling over conundrums. Darling, I hope you have got on well, not particularly from my point of view, but because I know you want to distinguish yourself. For my part I wish that you had nothing to turn to but me, so that there would be no lure to take you from me. No, I don't wish that at all. I wish that you may have all the kingdoms of the world before you, for I know that even then you will come to your laddie. Girl, I am only writing this nonsense to cheer you up in case you are in the dumps to-night. I always was after those big exams, but you are such a charming little philosopher that you may escape a bad mood.

By the way I think I told you that I had purchased a wooden implement called a 'baffie'. I took it out for a round of golf with the redoubtable John Stevenson yesterday, and by its aid I vanquished him *Laus Deo!* For he had been blowing about the thorough mauling I was to get. The one fault of the baffie is that it digs the ground a bit. I have therefore added a new beatitude, to wit - 'Blessed are they that hunger and thirst after a baffie, for they shall inherit the earth!' Dash it, I must buck into this sermon for it has to be squibbed off to-night. I fear it is going to be very bad. Let's hope it will not be hissed off. All my love and all my thoughts, dearest Jess.

Ever your Boy

Don't reply to this. See you Sunday sure!

5 Wilton Mansions

9th June 1914

My darling

This is to be just a scrawl, for I am fallen on a busy hour. I have been attempting to write a sermon all morning, and it hath not prospered - also I have to leave shortly for that bally funeral - hence the scramble. I had a fine day's golf yesterday - a foursome on Sandyhills - two rounds. My partner and I won both games - one up and five up and three - a most successful day. But one has to pay for these slack times. I am glad you are having a good time. That would be the only thing that would reconcile one to this separation. Dear it's the 9th - and good old *Mr T Empus is fugiting*. Go canny with that bathing in the cold water, and look out for cramp. It's the devil when the temperature gets low. Sutherland comes thro' to-morrow. I'll enclose his amusing postcard. He is fearfully bucked over his MA. Poor old chap, he has had to serve a long apprenticeship for it. I'll write you a decent letter soon. Keep the tryst at the Frog Rock. All my love, girl.

Yours,

Hugh

5 Wilton Mansions

N Kelvinside

30th June 1914

Dearest Jess

I guess you couldn't manage yesterday. We waited from ten to half past twelve, and Nan was groaning. However I defended your character against all and sundry - declaring you had never failed me yet save for a mighty good reason. I fear I won't get a letter from you for a day or two. That fool Jane forgot to notify the post-office of our return and this morning's letters are on the way to Largo.

Tim is to be here till Thursday or Friday, and he confided to me that he was going out to see you. He was very dumped when I said he couldn't. But next time, nothing on earth will hinder him from interviewing you. He has got a bit of a cold, and that is a bad point with him, but Davidson reckoned it wasn't much. We are going out to golf this afternoon, and then for a long evening in Dennistoun working off arrears. Things have got badly muddled, and I'm going to have a game sorting them.

All my love, darling, and go warily.

Your boy

Thunderguy, Pirnmill, Isle of Arran July 1914

Reid family group, Pirnmill 1914 with Jessie front left

Chapter 8

"It comes to me that you and I made our best friendship under the shadow. Some day we shall read them over together and perhaps we shall find, as I did, that our eyes grow full of unashamed tears."

Two major events were to change the course of Hugh and Jessie's lives in the summer of 1914: war and pregnancy.

Jessie returns to Pirnmill on the Isle of Arran while Hugh remains in Glasgow which in July of that year played host to King George V and Queen Mary. Although there are indications in Hugh's letters that Jessie might be pregnant, it is not entirely clear if her condition has been confirmed to Hugh until August or September. However about the middle of July Hugh refers to a "debacle" after which there is an element of stress evident in his letters. The letters written from "Remote", the farm on which his brother works and at which Hugh must have spent some days at intervals between the end of July and the end of September, are undated.

North Kelvinside

1st July 1914

Dearest Jess

I was tremendously bucked to get your letter this morning, for I was sure that it would go to Largo. It was rather disappointing that you didn't get in, but I knew there was a reason. You should be a very cheery crowd down there, and I am hoping you will have a desperate good time.

Well, dear, Tim and I were out golfing yesterday, and we squared the match on the last green - both round in 88. This was not too bad considering I had not been doing anything at Connell, and Tim had been at it day and night. It was rather wet when we finished, so we dropped in to Jarvie's and were there most of the night. I had one or two calls to make, so I left Tim to go home, but when I returned he was sitting playing cards with them. They are a most hospitable gang. I'll give your message to Nancy, when I see her next, and attend to Para Handy. I haven't had a look round my shelves yet. I believe we might go to worse places than just old Pirnmill for our honeymoon. But certainly it must be θαλασσα.* I'm just going over to see Lewis Sutherland - I think I told you that he had got through his Nat.Phil. at last. I am just wondering what it will be like when old Tim goes away. The place is getting mighty empty all round. My dearest love to you, lass.

Your boy

The sea

N. Kelvinside
3rd July 1914

Darling Jess

Your dear letter made me wish most terribly to be with you. I don't understand those seedy turns of yours, and they are very worrying. What is it you feel? Pain anywhere? Giddiness? Tell me girl all about it: because it is uncertainty that is most trying. I am in that hopelessly love-lorn state when I envy the blades of grass you step on. I don't know how much time I, not waste, but spend thinking about little you. Jess my dearest, don't you wish our time had come! I am sitting looking over old Glasgow, and its roofs are not inspiring. Would that they were in some magical way transformed into the Frog Rock. The decorations are going up for the King's visit, and tawdriness and cheap colour is everywhere.

I had my mission meeting last night. I think my folks were glad to see me back. They said so anyhow. It was cheery getting all my lads and lassies round me again. The Thursday meeting is off during July; however I offered to go on with their singing lessons, so next Thursday I have them from 7.45 to 10. Trip is on Saturday of which you shall hear anon. I am looking forward to it with no particular joy. Tim is going back home to-day, so we shall be alone in our glory - and desolation. I had two nice rounds of golf with him. We squared the first on the last green, and I won the second by two up. I must get busy on a sermon.

I get your kisses every night, dear. Do you get mine? They carry all my heart.

For another little while, dearest,

Your boy

5 Wilton Mansions
Sunday afternoon

Darling

I am just going to write a wee note, as I am beastly fagged, and propose to go to bed for the afternoon. We had the trip yesterday, and I have not had such a violent time for months. Mercifully the weather was good; we spent the day doing energetic things like football, rounders, and a thousand other strenuosities. This morning I had a throat like a crow, and my legs wouldn't work. However I had to make some kind of shape at the morning service. But if you had been there, you would have disowned me.

Glasgow is very busy just now, and an appalling number of ugly decorations are waving. I wish I could get out of it all and down to you. Dear, I'm stuck; my eyes are going together, and the pen wandereth whither it listeth. If you were here you would order me to stop writing, and come and rest in your arms; and I'm just going to do it. Have you had any more seedy turns? Please tell me exactly.

Heart's love to you, little wife.

N Kelvinside
6th July 1914

My darling Jess

I begin to admire your sticking out powers more and more. It is only the 6th of the month, and I am longing and wearying for the end of it. I can't bear to think of the long weeks and the endless days till I see you again. You are interfering badly with my sleep. Last night I had four hours in the dark trying to get to sleep in spite of you. My only pleasure is ticking off the days each morning. Girl, I can't tell you the strength of my love for you. Nothing seems worth while if you are not in it. The morning has come grey and wet, and there is not much to do. I must just stand in to work again till I am tired enough to sleep.

The trip on Saturday was enormously successful from one point of view. The old folks sat on the shore, ate and watched the ships go up and down. The young ones, and I was dragged into this, sported on the darned links till they could hardly stand, and then said that they had enjoyed it fine. Did I tell you all this yesterday? I remember writing, but I was so all out that I have no idea what I said. There was another service last night, which I had to take - Johnston's Mission. Bad air, gassy smell (not from me) and a bang of people - result - fed up to the neck.

I was sorry to hear about Nina's misfortune. A poisoned foot should be cross-stitched in crochet-work lingerie and served with red-cross jelly salad. It is as sore as the devil with his best silver-mounted suiner-stirring horns on. Well, it's no good gittering on like this, Jess. You aren't telling me how you are. All my love and all my thoughts.

Your boy

5 Wilton Mansions
North Kelvinside
Tuesday 11.30 pm - bed

Dearest Jess

I have just been re-re-re-reading that darling long letter you wrote on the wet Sunday. Do I seem selfish if I wish a few more of the same wetness. It was just you to write a three-page letter when your finger was still sore - as, reading between the lines I have no doubt it was. What grand news that you are keeping fitter. Dear, it has been worrying me frightfully that you were unwell, and that I was not there to kiss it better. I hope to heaven there will be no more.

Hope your royal procession processes all right. You must tell me. I suppose Papa and Mama would be Him an' Her. Were you Princess Mary? I have dodged Royalty to-day most successfully. To begin with I slept in badly - got up at 11.30. (Please teacher, I was visiting in Dennistoun the day before). I had a leisurely *déjeuner*, and proceeded to Central Station to catch the 2.2 to (no more 2's) East Kilbride. Got out in about an hour (the train visits most of the Glasgow suburbs en route) and met Willie Johnston. The whole family...(pause to slay a night-moth, which is dancing round my candle) have taken a lovely farm-house there. Played two rounds of golf, had a slight motor-run, then home towards nine. Mater got a ticket from Mrs Duff for the *varsity* grounds, and had a great view of everything. The King and Queen looked bored, but Princess Mary was rather sweet. I have had a fearful day of hay fever, and it got so bad that I went to bed whenever I came in. I can see a little now, but for about an hour I was almost blind. It is a cruel thing, and one can get nothing to soften it down.

I had a hefty day of visitation yesterday. Saw the Jarvies - also your postcard - that infernal Island of Arran thing, to which I object most violently. One of my little choir girls has pneumonia, and nothing would serve but an unvarnished and lengthy account of the beastly trip - a cursed nuisance. Then I struck a house of mourning, and was let in for an unlooked for funeral on Thursday. So one is never finished. I haven't had a moment to start a sermon for Sunday and it is almost Wednesday.

My darling wee lassie, how we love each other, don't we? I'm thinking, thinking about you all the day, and I've come to the only serious conclusion that I ever reached in my life - that I couldn't live without you, and that I wouldn't even care to try. Dear, take care of yourself, for you guard two lives - yours and mine - neither of much use without the other, but together - a home and a stronghold.

Jess girl, much thought of you maketh me wild - and my remarks become more than incoherent. Perhaps laughter is best. Good-night, darling wife. I'm going to blow out the candle, and think of you again and again. Always your lover,
Hugh

5 Wilton Mansions
11th July 1914

My dearest

I am slowly recovering my temper, but you cannot expect an experience like that without bitterness to follow. It was such cruel fortune. Everything went against us all day, and that final little effort of fate finished it. I am very anxious to hear about your toothache. It would soon spoil your holiday if you allowed it to go on unchecked. It seems that an angry devil is pursuing your tired body, but cheers little one. He shall not have your spirit while I hold its key.

Sutherland came thro' last night, very cheerful. We went to some alleged Society Entertainers in Kelvingrove Park. I kept wondering what level of society they had been in the habit of entertaining, for their songs were frequently vulgar, and their jokes weak as a new born kitten. However it passed the time.

And now, beloved, I have turned my calendar to the magic numbers - 11-7-14. Give you joy - and a kiss for it. Nineteen isn't a very advanced age, but I've just been reading a novel which states that a girl wakens when she is eighteen - also that for her there are three mountains - born, loved, died - each of which rises but once. Does it, girl? The middle term I mean. My darling, you know I have given all my heart to you, and I know that I hold yours in safe keeping. Let us live to love, so I guess shall our days be long upon the earth. I'm sure that love like ours is the perpetual elixir of life. God speed you, beloved, on your twentieth course, and bring you nearer to the big day. My love more than ever.

Hugh

5 Wilton Mansions

13th July 1914

Dearest

I haven't yet heard from you since the debacle, so I don't know your views on it. I only hope that at least the toothache is better. We have had brother Sutherland since Friday, and there has been much laughter, and little slumber. We had a strenuous day yesterday. It was most dreadfully stuffy work preaching, and we were completely done up. I had the 11 o'clock in Wellpark, he had the 2 o'clock: while I also had his 2 o'clock in Govan. Then we halved the Mission at night. I took first part - including the accompaniment to a solo which he sang, and he did the spouting. Both fed up this morning. He leaves soon for Cumnock, then he has a fortnight at Stranraer with his girl!!! Alas, for us. I have to rush off at once to the Royal Infirmary. I have a message that one of our members had a shock, and is in a precarious condition. So are my nerves! No more à *ce moment* dearest love, Jess.

Yours,

Hugh

N Kelvinside

21st July 1914

My own Jess

I have just come in from Edinburgh to receive your letter of Sunday. Thanks, darling. My heart has a nasty way of jumping when it sees your calligraphy, and really I can't blame it, for I jump myself. Glad that your toothache is away. I assume it is, since you don't mention it. I have had a very jolly day of golf. I went thro' by a special train which took no notice of any stations by the way, and adjourned with my uncle to Barnton. A rare golfing lunch in the club-house, and then two rounds. They insisted on keeping me till this morning, so I just scrambled home in time for dinner. Now I have to sit down and write a sermon, oh bitter fortune! I had this note from the bishop of Lansdowne. I accepted the engagement, as it may lead to that which you know. But I shall be in a most dreadful funk that day. It will be quite the biggest job I ever tackled. Don't say anything about this supply.

Of course I agree with you about solitary holidays - indeed when you come to think of it, how few things we differ about. But the game is hopeless when you have two sets of people with different ideas and ideals trying to trip it beneath one roof. *Née*. It can't be done. It certainly ain't in our case. For if I got the choice of a mansion and company and a barrel alone, I vow we should choose the barrel - and be jolly happy too. Glad Hector and Alison are enjoying life. I guess you will feel a bit green occasionally. I do.

All my love, dearest. This blessed sermon waits tapping on my conscience's door.
Your Hugh

5 Wilton Mansions
5.30 a.m. 22nd July 1914

My woman

I'm not going to write you a letter of news. I got up at this amazing hour to tell you a few things which occurred to me in the watches of the night. It fell that as I was casually reading some of your old letters to me by dim candle-light and I believe steadfastly that love-letters should always be so read - that I came upon some written from Pirnmill at this time last year, and they were so lovely, so full of pain and heartening that I felt drawn to you by a thousand chains of gold. It comes to me that you and I made our best friendship under the shadow. Some day we shall read them over together, and perhaps we shall find, as I did, that our eyes grow full of unashamed tears. You may fancy dimly how you helped me through it all, but you shall never know quite what your love and your courage did for me, when everything was grey. I remember clearly how, heart-sick and hopeless, I would wake of a morning, weary and heavy laden, if ever son of man was, and how even your hand-writing on an envelope would tell out the old *'Courage, mon ami!'* and cheer me to a better than my poor best. Such memories are an abiding possession, and I gladly give to you the service of my life - a small thing, but my best gift.

We have come through fair and foul weather, hands held, and I have a passionate certainty that you are the only woman in the world to whom I can give my love, and find it in the end glorified. My dearest love, it is long since you spoke to me in deeper tones than your own beauty. You are lovely. Your eyes bend on me sometimes so that I cannot speak for joy and terror. I love every waving hair of your head. But I have learned to value even more the brave heart I know, and the clear shining of a soul that does not turn back. You are all woman to me, yet you are more than woman. For here is that in the call of your arms which breaks my native reserve towards women, and carries me forward to a greater love. In these days that wonderful compelling love of yours is to me the great reality. It is the sorest thought of my heart that my dear father did not live to bid us love. I know how his great soul would have welcomed you, and how keenly he would have courted the love of his son's lass, and it takes little persuading to feel his presence and hear his kindly benediction. I fancy him saying in words written by another big soul, "Beloved, let us love one another: for love is of God; and every one that loveth is born of God, and knoweth God". Jess I know our love is of that greatness, and we may follow without fear where it leads. The steps of the early passers are changing. First they were at long intervals as though hopeless men went to a long slavery; now they are frequent and cheerful, as of men who go out hearty and content with their breakfast and their God - two entities which we hold too far apart.   And so I change my pen, and give you good speed of the last week of separation. So only that it bring you health and hale thought and the happiness of well filled minutes and at the last, turn you to me, I have little quarrel with it. My dearest love, fare thee well. I think all is summed up to your seeing eyes if I write but this, "I love you".

Ever your husband

Remote

Ford

Midlothian

Tuesday night

Dearest Jess

I have a lonely thought - I write from bed, when most of the household has retired, and Tim is not yet in from some midnight *amour*. I expect him every moment with a warm tale of *derring-do*. The wind has been soughing round the house and among the trees, and it would be all right in summer. But it's rather mournful and depressing when one is a hundred miles from the Lady of Dreams. Thank God I'll be back on Thursday. I'll see you at Craig's on Friday!!! Tim is in good form. He's going in to Edinburgh to-morrow to his class, and he will post this: so you ought to get it to-morrow night.

Darling - there is an old couple here, a most peaceful pair of little doves. I hope we shall be like them when the years have done their *darndest* on us. Am I incoherent and illogical in my sequence of thought? But so would you be if you were in love with the dearest and bonniest lass in the wide world. Extra special edition - 'she loves me too!' We had a clerical party here last night. The U.F. man and his wife and the Old Kirk[11] and his wife and his ma-in-law. The U.F. lad a decent buck, but the O.K. the limit. Tim has been *trothing* the local beauties out (female ones) but I have no confessions to make. It's almighty funny how we've changed ends so far as that is concerned. At first I had all the *deviltries* to own up to - now it's a monologue from you. As I grow faithful, you grow false! Maybe.

Here's Tim, so the game's up. I gave him your love, and he is returning his to you. He has the infernal cheek to mention kisses. I reply that I shall attend to that part of it.

All my love, dearest lass. Yours always,

Hugh

Remote

Ford

Tuesday

My dearest

I have been looking for a chance to write you for some time now, and this is really the first. It has been a case of running about from one place to another for the last three days. Let me tell you of it. Tim and I left here on Saturday morning at 7.30 - a beastly cold journey in the motor down to Dalkeith. Got home about 10.30 and had a long crack with mother. Met a gang of relatives at 2.45: then out to the church. Service[12] was trying, especially for mother. An apology for absence was read among others from your pater. Then a long wait at the cemetery in cold weather, a dim sight of your home for all practical purposes a thousand miles away, and home. Back to Edinburgh by the 8.20 and down to Newhaven Road - mother, Tim, Uncle John and myself. Week-end there - twice at church on Sunday - morning, St. George's, Dr. Jowett of New York preaching - evening, New North, Slater. Enjoyed both services immensely. Out here Monday afternoon, and turned on to cut the grass, which filled up the time till supper and bed. So you will forgive my silence, since it was a case of bitter constraint and sad occasion dear.

I was fearfully glad to get your letters last night and this morning. How often have I told you that you are a perfect darling! Dearest, I am glad you are not worrying, and I am certain that it will be all right. I've listened to a lot of talk about circumstances ruling folks, but I still believe in the old doctrine that a man can be master and not slave of circumstance. If things won't go right, we shall make them. And these are not simply pious words without meaning, for I have been thinking much about ourselves, and have much to say to you when I see you. Meantime, keep up your heart, and get thro' that exam. Think of nothing but that; I'll do the rest of the thinking for us both. Dear, I'm so glad you love me, for love means faith if it means anything, and faith means winning through everything. Else is my philosophy a pack of cards. I'll ride over to Pathhead and post this that it may get to you to-night. All my love, my own wife.

Yours, H

Remote

Sunday

My dearest

Here is a fine autumn Sunday morning with the sun streaming thro' the window and the birds singing in the trees. I have yet an hour before we leave for church and you shall have it. On a day like this it is impossible to believe that things can go wrong with our love, and I am certain that all is right. If I get any meaning at all from nature it is that the big things, life and love, go on - that there is a real immortality of principle. Darling, let us love. In a week I shall see you and kiss you again. Isn't it great? We have been very busy these last days securing the harvest, and now all is safely gathered in. Two days threshing next week will finish it. Mother is coming out to-morrow afternoon in Uncle Tom's car. She has been enjoying her Edinburgh visit *Al*. I had a p.c. from Johnnie McKenzie. He and Simpson and Weir have joined Lochiel's Camerons and they are now at Aldershot. I wish I could go also. Isn't it hard lines that one should have a thorn in one's flesh? I got notice yesterday that my exam is on October 1st - Thursday week I think. Still I haven't done much work, but I am going to start seriously this week. It is all very well slacking: Up to a point it is pleasant, for one seems to defy circumstances in an exhilarating way; but exams are for getting thro', and there is an end of it. I hope you have the best of luck with yours dear. I know how you have worked, and if ever anyone does, you deserve to get through. It is certain, however, you will never stumble. You used to kid me that you had no brains, but you never succeeded in deceiving me. The thing was too obvious. Good luck then my dear. I shall think of you all the time. I hear them getting ready and I must close up. All my love, my own darling Jess.

Yours,

Hugh

Remote

Monday night

Darling

I have not long arrived, and I hurry to write you. I had your note this morning. Keep up your heart, little one. I guess it will be all right. At the worst, I have a plan, which needs talking face to face. It is very peaceful here to-night, and one can hardly realise that there are shadows in life. My woman, we shall stand by each other through whatever length of days is given us. The main thing at present seems to me to be that this should be absolutely between ourselves, and so your part - the harder - is to be perfectly natural. All my love is yours, and all my thoughts gather about you just now. I have no liberty to write more just now. I am glad to get a holiday in any event, as whatever may be before us, health is *primus inter pares*.

Good-night, sweet heart, Your man

PART II

New Army Camps: October 1914 - July 1915

August 1914 from *Yuletide Greetings from the Cameron Highlanders* sent
to Jessie, Christmas 1918

Wedding of Alison Reid (Jessie's sister) and Hector Hetherington, 28 March 1914. Jessie is the bridesmaid next to Hector. Hugh is immediately behind her. Other members of Jessie's family in the middle row are Howard, Jessie's brother, and Winnie, her sister (second and third from left); behind and between Jessie and Hector stands Arnold, Jessie's older brother. Her father, William Reid is to the extreme right. In the front row are Dine, Jessie's young sister, Alan, the youngest and seated next to him is Jessie Hunter Reid, Jessie's mother.

Clouds of war hung over Europe in the summer of 1914. Following the assassination of Archduke Franz Ferdinand in Sarajevo on 28 June the most powerful nations launched offensives with the intention of defeating their enemies quickly but by the autumn of 1914 all of these offensives had failed. When Germany invaded Belgium to gain access to France, Britain declared war on Germany on 4 August thus joining in a war that came to be known as The Great War or The First World War. As the first regular troops of the British Expeditionary Force embarked for France and Belgium they expected to be home for Christmas. No one in the autumn of 1914 would have believed that few would return and that by Armistice Day on 10 November 1918, only four years later, a total of 8,020,780 men from the Allied and Axis troops would have lost their lives and 21,228,813 others would have been left wounded or maimed for life.

Two million men volunteered their services as a result of Lord Kitchener's appeal for his New Army. Many were young and eager for an opportunity to spend some time away from home. Others were motivated by patriotism or a desire to fight injustice. At stirring meetings in Glasgow and Inverness, Colonel D W Cameron of Lochiel called on young Scots to enlist with the Cameron Highlanders. Bold posters with the call to "Join Lochiel's Camerons" appeared on Glasgow trams. Within a few weeks the 5th and 6th Battalions of "Lochiel's Camerons" were formed and sent direct to Aldershot and as recruits continued to arrive at the recruitment centre at an old hotel in Glasgow's West George Street, another battalion was formed. From West George Street these young men, many of whom were students or young professionals, were marched daily, headed by a piper, to the Inverness train which would take them to their new headquarters at Cameron Barracks.

No military glamour awaited these young recruits in Inverness. On arrival they had to sleep on the dark and rat-infested stone floor of the Milburn Distillery and wash in the burn or mill-dam. But the rigours of the two months spent by the men in Inverness were lightened by the hospitality of many kind inhabitants who supplied porridge and milk to supplement their meagre rations, placed private bathrooms at their disposal and offered them the peace and comfort of sitting-rooms for letter-writing and clothes-drying. Uniforms were not yet available for the young men and many hired kilts from some willing regular soldiers at the barracks to avoid the shame of going on leave in their "civvies".

On 8 October 1914, Lieutenant-Colonel D P Haig was gazetted as the first commanding officer of the 7th Battalion and on the 30 November the battalion left Inverness for further training at Aldershot. In a letter to Colonel Haig, the Provost of Inverness paid tribute to the men who had "by their exemplary conduct, and their manly and courteous bearing, won favour on all hands."

The battalion, consisting of 1136 men, spent Christmas and New Year in the Salamanca Barracks at Aldershot in Hampshire as a unit of the 44th Brigade, 15th Scottish Division.

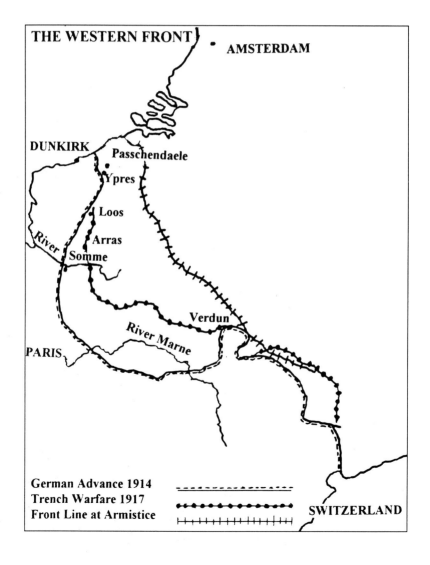

Chapter 1

"God help us, Jess. Are we never to be together?"

Hugh and Jessie were married in a registry office at 4 Minerva Street in the "District of Anderston in the Burgh of Glasgow" on the 15 October 1914. The very same day Hugh signed his name in the recruiting register for Lochiel's Camerons and headed north to Inverness the following day while Jessie travelled to Sheffield to her sister and brother-in-law a few days later. Jessie was nineteen and had recently completed her first year at the University of Glasgow while Hugh was twenty-four and in the final year of his Divinity course at the United Free Church College.

To what extent Hugh's decision to enlist with the Cameron Highlanders was influenced by the need, in an age still dominated by Victorian attitudes, to provide a cover for his hasty marriage because of Jessie's condition is not clear. What is clear however is the pressure being brought to bear on both Hugh and Jessie to keep secret, not just Jessie's pregnancy, but their marriage as well.

The unpredicted developments of October 1914 put an end to Hugh's near-completed studies for church ministry, and Jessie's university studies.

Hugh's name on the recruitment register of Lochiel's Camerons and an extract from Hugh and Jessie's marriage certificate, both dated 15 October 1914.

Inverness

22 October 1914

Dearest Jess

I had your letter with all the enclosures and it was grand to get them. It was like a message from the promised land. I agree absolutely with your decision to go to Sheffield. It is fine of Hector and Alison to write as they do, and I am happy to think that you are in such good hands. Inverness is impossible. So many people here are dead keen to know you, which will come in good time - also when the day's work is over, I am very tired. Let me have your Sheffield address when you get there.

I have struck some weird society since I arrived. The mildest swear is 'bloody' - repeated in every sentence - and the range and variety is immense. It has cured me of all desire to swear. Honestly it is rather fierce being with these people day and night, and sleep is an escape. The work has been heavy lately - squad drill for seven hours. On Monday night we had out-post work in the dark - the only exciting thing so far.

I've been getting a lot of letters. I enclose you one from Emmy Neil, and return you Hector's and Alison's. I also had word from them. I'll show you them some day. Don't return Emmy's.

I'm now going down town. We have long leave to-night, which means we don't need to be in till eleven. I'm going to the Neils for a bath and a feed. There are a whole lot of things I want to tell you, but my head is not very clear.

All my love and thoughts,

Ever your boy

The sergeant in charge of our squad said that another chap - a nice fellow - and I had the "only damned brains in the bloody squad" and he has stuck us in the front to keep the others right. Eh what?

Depot

Inverness

Tuesday

Dearest Jess

I have a very hard letter to write. Leave has been cancelled and we are not to get off. Even if we had, we could not have been together in Glasgow. Uncle John was in, and mother and he wrote me - both saying it would be most indiscreet. God help us, Jess. Are we never to be together? I'm going to refuse all leave now, and stay by the regiment. Nothing seems any damned good - to tell you the truth I'm heart sick. Uncle J and mother were troubled about the Jarvies knowing. They ask me to counsel you to keep the secret of our hasty marriage very carefully. I fancy I don't need to. Well, darling, I'm sore, and hurt, and bitter - mostly for your suffering - but neither persons nor circumstances can touch our love by so much as a breath. Thank God for that. That's all dearest, and mercifully that's all that matters. My love to you most precious one. Ever your,

Husband

Inverness

Saturday

My darling

Your letter was hard reading: I could see you crying in the darkness, and my own helplessness to aid you is cruel. But I know you too well to fear that you will not endure our separation - however long it may be. For my part I regard it as part of the price we have to pay and the way we pay will fix the happiness afterwards. For altho' the weeks and months seem long just now, I never let myself forget the long years before us when we shall be together. It is also much happiness to me to remember the short hour in the 'servatory the night we said good-bye. Whenever I am dead down, I think of that and I can see you and touch you, kiss you, put my arms about you. My dear, I can at this moment catch the brush of your hair on my face. Think of these things, dearest of all, and courage! I did not quite see the Glasgow business as mother did, but you and I are going to fall in with every one of her wishes. If I get leave from Inverness I shall go to her. If we are sent to Aldershot and I get leave from there I shall go to Sheffield. The best reason for such a decision is the mere expense. I am living on 4/- a week, and you can't make expensive railway journeys on that. Also there is the time spent in travelling.

Remember your promise to me dear - to keep cheery for the sake of our baby. I know how you feel and feel very bitter and crushed - but stick it. I have my work up here, and it is so exhausting that I haven't much spare energy for thinking and sorrowing. It is worse for you, but you know I always maintained that in the last resort you were the stronger. Help me to keep that belief strong and clean.

And now about things regimental. There is a strong rumour that we are to be sent to Cairo, and they expect trouble there. But no one really knows. The work has been stiff, and most parts of me have gone wrong - indigestion, left foot leader, and rather worse, a slight rupture. But I have kept out of the hospital so far, and I'm all right now. I was playing accompaniments for my chum, Fred Pidwell, last night at the big Belgian Fund concert. He got *encored* each time and sang best of anyone there. I'll send you a report of it when I get a newspaper. Now darling, write me soon again. You are very good to me, and I read and re-read you letters. I'm doing my damnedest to keep the flag flying, and it's going to stay up. I know well that you will never let it down. 'Bye just now, dearest wife.

Ever and ever your boy

Depot
27th October 1914

My darling wife

I have both your letters from Sheffield. Do I require to say how happy I was to get them? That would surely be padding. My thoughts have been all of you lately for I know pretty well what you are going thro'. Mercifully it is only a shadow, but it has been dark at times. Be sure lass that I will come to you as soon as I can, but I am now a man under authority, and I've just to take what is going. Dear, how I should love to kiss those little clothes you are making for our baby. I hope, oh so much, that I will get to you before it comes. I knew Hector and Alison would be good to you. Will you read them such parts of my letters as you think fit.

I am glad to say I have kept out of hospital so far. I'm not pretending it was easy, but I've done it. I got my foot well bandaged, and it has been easier to-day. We did not go the route march as we were not reckoned fit. I was some glad. We have been squad drilling and so forth. I got put forward a section for knowing my drill, so I am not with quite so many goats. That's no little comfort! Last night we were judging distances by rifle-shot in the dark. It was quite exciting. The night marching is fine. You hear the tramp-tramp without seeing anything, and it stirs one's blood. I think they are putting back-bone into me. They are certainly straightening the one I've got.

Now about finance, dearest. You haven't said anything to me, and I'd like you to. I have a letter from mother and I quote her words. "You must let me know what I am to do about money. Uncle John said that if Jessie did not want it at once, he will put it into your PO Savings Bank Account, £6 at the end of this month, £2 for the last half of this month and £4 in advance for November. Or she may want some of it and in that case the rest of it could be put to your account. It will all depend upon what arrangement she makes with the Hetheringtons. Her separation allowance will be enough if they don't charge board and my £1 would be added regularly to your account. These are merely suggestions which you may or may not carry out. I am anxious to save a little money for you both. The future is unknown." That is all I know, and the whole decision is with you, girl. Two things I want to make clear. That Hector must not be out of pocket on our account and that you must not be short. This last is an order. Let me know whatever you decide - if you feel you want advice, consult Hector. But remember, I'd rather send you my whole pay than even suspect that you were stinting. The one would be far sorer on me than the other. Now, darling, I send you all the love that I bear you - guess it.

Ever your husband

Depot
Inverness

Sunday

Dearest wife

Thanks ever so much for your letter. I believe you are committing the unheard of offence of writing love letters to your husband after marriage. I can't tell you how happy I am when I see your hand on an envelope. My heart jumps in the old way - only with a new strength. I am sure you are doing right about the finances - only see that you get the separation allowance. I am reduced in pay to 4/- so you ought to get something extra. I'm managing fine on my slender screw - and it is a very educating experience to keep a watch on one's pennies and good for the soul.

I have been all right this last week as far as my feet are concerned. The indigestion has been off and on, sometimes rather bad. However I guess it will come right soon. I'm getting into fine form, and you won't know me when I come home. The latest rumour is that in a fortnight we are to get long leave - Friday to Tuesday and after that to Aldershot. I'm hoping it's not true. If the weekend is right, I think I shall spend it with mother in Edinburgh or Glasgow. For two reasons. I haven't the money to take me to Sheffield and the time would be very short. The other and the strong reason is that mother is just breaking her heart about me, and as we are young and as we have done the hurt, I feel that no sacrifice is to be shirked if by any means we may bring comfort. If you want me at Sheffield in face of that I will still come, and don't hesitate to speak frankly. Of course the whole thing is just a rumour at present. If I am going to Aldershot, it will be in a draft and I will not see you. It's pretty rough luck for us both, as, my darling, I'm just aching to see you - to touch you, to put my arms round you and hold you so close. But this is the way we have made and we must walk it, even tho' it cuts our feet. I must write to mother now but I won't say anything about the week-end till I hear from you. I can't write anything about our baby. My head is just buzzing round about over it. Sometimes I'm glad, sometimes I'm scared - for you. For God's sake, careful darling - what are a hundred babies to your life. I'm getting incoherent so it's time to shut down.

My dear love to you my wife.

Ever your boy

Salamanca Barracks
Sunday

My own darling

I am spending Sunday afternoon in my bed. There is not much to do when you are off duty, and my bunk has a charm of its own, to wit, privacy. Also it is the warmest place in barracks. Now I have a big subject to write you about. I would to

God I could talk it to you with my arms about you. But let's pretend - kiss first? Right. Low let's be serious. Mother wrote me a long letter and the burden of it is that it would be most indiscreet for you to go to Edinburgh. My people are well known there to a great number of people, and it is much too near Glasgow. Mother wants me to impress upon you the absolute need for caution, lest our secret should be known; she says it would simply wreck our future - as indeed it would. It is of you and our baby I am thinking, dear. So you see, tho' you might prefer Edinburgh, you will be safer in Sheffield. They suggest that you go into a nursing home there, and mother will pay all expenses. I hope you will see that this is best and right. Mother says, "It is just keeping the truth hidden that carries me through these black days, and if it leaked out, for me it would be the end." So Jess, don't feel as tho' you were being made a shuttle-cock, but believe in our ideas for you, and above all in my absolute devotion to your interests and your life. I love you, my darling, as I love nothing on earth: if you are sad, I am sad; if you are happy, I am happy. My whole life is just to serve you, and nothing counts before that. Another, and a reason of our very own for staying in Sheffield, is that I am almost certain to get leave at the end of this month, and I'm coming straight to you. I can do it much easier and quicker if you are in Sheffield. Now here is another thing. If you are staying on with Hector and Alison, we will both feel more independent and better if board were paid for you, say a small sum like 10/- a week - all we can afford - and yet something to make you feel that you are not on the charity stunt. I want you to speak to them about it: put it as nicely as you can and I know how nice that is - say - it is not the question of expense to them, also that nothing on earth can repay their kindness and love, but that it is for our sakes. Mother will send you the 10/- weekly out of the £1. She wanted to send me the other 10/- for food and so on, but I won't have it, for I don't really need it. Again you will never tell me about your share of the separation allowance, and I want to know. Are you getting it regularly? I am quite comfortable here, if I knew that you were right. Oh for ten minutes talk with you. I could make it all so much clearer. My hearty love to you, sweetheart.

Your husband

Chapter 2

"Hugh and she may have been foolish: but neither is capable of serious wrong: and I would not have Jessie for anything feel that we, who love her most, have anything but affection and gratitude for her." (Hector Hetherington)

The two letters which follow shed some light on Hugh and Jessie's predicament brought about by Jessie's pregnancy and their hasty marriage. The first letter, from Hector, is addressed to Jessie's father, William Reid, while Alison's letter is to her mother. Alison Reid, Jessie's older sister and Hector Hetherington were married in March 1914 and it is with them that Jessie is living in Sheffield at this point.

Sheffield

9th December 1914

My dear Papa

It is a matter of considerable difficulty to write clearly on the problem you presented in your letter. Alison and I have talked things over: and Jessie and she have also discussed things. I did not join in that discussion; and thought Jessie would speak her mind more freely to Alison.

The difficulty that I find in this matter is that it would be very unfortunate if any bad feeling arose between Hugh and his relatives. I should do much to avoid a quarrel with my people: and I should regret it in my case and therefore for that reason <u>and that reason only,</u> I would be willing to consult the feelings of the Manns. But their attitude in this matter is wrong in principle: and though I should be anxious to keep peace on all sides it seems to me that to acquiesce in their wishes now is to admit their right to the position that they take up.

So far as I understand the situation, they desire not to acknowledge Jessie until some undefined future: and meantime they want the whole business kept quiet. I will not comment on the obvious lack of charity in their views. The only point that concerns <u>us</u> is the plain impracticability of the whole proposal. 1. For to begin with, Hugh is not the only person in the world with friends. Jessie's friends have missed her out of her ordinary activities, and some of them, I expect, know why. So that whether Hugh's friends know of his marriage or not, some of her friends are bound to know: and such news as that does not need long to travel. 2. What is to be the situation <u>after</u> the war is over: and Hugh and Jessie have definitely to face their future together? Hugh can't go back to the U.F. Hall as if nothing had happened. And whatever is decided upon then, means the open acknowledgement of the whole thing. Now it is folly for the Manns to pretend that

that acknowledgement will be easier then than now. It will be very much harder. And much the best thing that can happen both for Jessie and for Hugh is that the truth should be known to all whom it concerns <u>now</u>. They are, at present, both of them in retirement from public notice: and people are thinking about other things. Hence, when they do begin their life to-gether, they will begin it naturally, and without exciting stares and comments and public notice. And added to this plain practical fact, there is the other issue, that to conceal things unnecessarily now is to build their future on a systematic deception. The results can only be bad.

I know the pain of the whole matter well enough. But whenever I knew of Mamie, I insisted that things should be done openly and above board. And that policy was the thing that saved their future, at least so far as it could be saved. I should insist on the same principle now. I should doubt very much whether, even if concealment now would certainly help Hugh later, it would be the right thing to do. But so far from helping Hugh later, it will be a much more serious disadvantage: and that, to my mind, settles the matter. It is perfectly clear - it is unpleasant to say it, but it is true - that the Manns are not consulting Hugh and Jessie's future welfare in their request for a change of plan. They are consulting simply their own feelings, and trying to run away from a situation which, however unpleasant for them, is a good deal more unpleasant for Jess and for you.

The long and the short of it is this. If Jessie does not go to Edinburgh, or carry out some other arrangement that is entirely convenient to her, she is suffering ostracism: and that not merely from her wide circle of friends, but from her own family. Only the gravest reasons could be sufficient for a penalty of that kind. She and you have suffered enough as it is, without any extra trouble. And so far from there being grave reasons for this course, there are grave reasons <u>against</u> it. I should be most unwilling, for Jessie's own sake, that her arrangements should undergo any change.

When you add to this the fact that the tender feelings of the Manns are in not the slightest danger of laceration, it seems to me that the case is complete. If my opinion were to have any weight in the situation at all, I should be emphatic on the side of the original plan.

That is the general situation as plainly as I can see it or put it. You will see that we do not think that Jessie should stay in Sheffield. And again, I think, the reasons are clear.

(1) So far as Alison cannot be with her, Jessie will be among strangers: and that is bad. Plainly Alison cannot always be beside her: for since we haven't a maid, the house and her social activities and her lessons to the Belgians pretty well occupy her.

(2) I should not like the intervening weeks between now and the time that Jessie goes into the Home. Not merely would it be difficult to have people coming freely

about the house: but I should not like the responsibility of it. Jessie is very fit and happy and healthy: and so far, it has been nothing but delightful to have her. But when the critical period comes nearer, I should certainly be uneasy. I'm certain that nothing will go wrong: but still, there are two totally inexperienced people dealing with the situation: and in spite of expert advice, I think it unfair both to Jessie and to us.

(3) What is to happen <u>once</u> the critical period is over? We could have Jessie here for a bit, possibly even until Easter. But we don't want that, except in case of necessity. For it means a considerable disturbance in the house: the filling of all our rooms, and the curtailment or cessation of our social experiences. Jessie will have to come North afterwards: and it is much more sensible that she should travel now.

(4) She herself does not want to stay: and that ought to settle it.

(5) Finally, (and perhaps unfairly) I rather resent that Jessie should have received a letter from Hugh today saying that he has heard from Edinburgh that it has been arranged that she should go into a nursing home in Sheffield. (It's not Hugh's fault. He has merely been told that from Edinburgh.) I think it would be just as well to let the Manns know from the start that Jessie will live her own life without their interference, and that if they are foolish enough to let their pride stand between them and Hugh, <u>her</u> friends will take a clearer and kinder view of the case.

Alison and I feel that to have Jessie with us after Xmas means a sacrifice of many social opportunities: and that is serious for two people who are just beginning to find their friends in a new city. If the sacrifice were going to serve any useful purpose, if it were going to relieve you and mamma of any anxiety, or trouble, or going to make things easier for Jessie, we should most willingly make it. But if it is going to serve no such purpose, and merely make things easier for some foolish people, we are unwilling. And the Manns have no right for the sake of their own wretched feelings, even if there were any danger of contact between Jessie and their friends, to make things harder for you, for her, and for all concerned. I feel very strongly on the matter; and to put it bluntly, I'd see them damned first.

I write absolutely freely: as you asked me. That is our view of the situation. I think they are trying to put Jessie in a very false position. Hugh and she may have been foolish: but neither of them is capable of serious wrong: and I would not have Jessie for anything feel that we, who love her most, have anything but affection and gratitude for her.

There may be some facts that I do not know, or have not grasped. If so, my judgement is open to modification. At present, I feel very like screwing Mr. John Clark's[13] precious neck.

Write us further what you decide. We are all fine. Much love from all three. Don't worry about this business. We'll run straight, and we'll run together: and it will be absolutely all right in the end.

Yours ever

Hector

P.S. At Jessie's request, I have written to Hugh, giving him my view of the case.

138 Graham Road

Ranmoor

Sheffield

December 11th

My eyes are nearly shut, Mama dear, but I'll stick them open for a moment or two. We have had another busy week of visitors, but I think we are round nearly everybody now. It's a blessing we have only once gone beyond tea for them else we'd be bankrupt - altho' it is a hefty tea most of them take. You should see how they make for Jessie's scones. Professor and Mrs Baker ate two platefuls yesterday, and Mrs Knoof did her best to annex the lot today. I can bake good cakes now - inexpensive ones, and as eggs are down to ten for 1/-, baking is possible.

Jessie and I played ourselves cutting a wee cream delaine frock today - and no, mother, we didn't cut the notches! I haven't forgotten the last notches I had to darn.

Best of thanks to Dad for sending on the book and for the Herald. Has Arnold been gazetted yet? Hector has seen the names of some Oxford friends in the Herald list of commissions.

It is a worrying, hard time for you, dear old Mama. It took Hector and me a long, long time to make up our minds what to do after Papa sent Mr. Clark's letter, and we're not finished wondering and thinking yet. But I think Hector is right in what he wrote to you. It means as much to both of us just now to get to know the University people here and they are beginning to treat us as friends. Next term I expect we shall have the younger men coming a good deal to the house, and Professor and Mrs. Green who live near us are particularly anxious to see something of us. You understand then why, if it is possible, we would rather be alone next term.

Hector too has got started to work of his own - and is writing good stuff. He needs quiet for that - and it is easier to say to you than to Dada, - that is one reason why we wait a little for our own children.

Still you know through everything, that should it mean a big help and saving of worry to you both, we shall keep Jessie here if other arrangements fail.

She is really content and happy, and was looking forward to going to Aunt Duncan and being near you. I hope that will still be possible.

Hector told you, I think, that Hugh is to have leave from January 4th to 11th. I feel that Jessie and he would be much happier seeing each other here, and I'd gladly stay and see that they had a holiday. Don't you think I should? Of course I miss seeing you all at Bertrohill, but I'll try and not weary till Easter - and then I'm hoping that one at least of you will be able to come for a bit of this holiday. Cook's people have not yet got details of the excursions, but Hector will probably go home on the 24th and return here before New Year's Day.

Is Winnie[14] having a share in the fairy play this week? How has she fared in the exams? I expect Dine[15] looks down on her altogether now. Tell Dine Hector is in need of her geometrical assistance tomorrow. He and Dr. Freund the German Prof are going for a walk, and must not go outside the five-mile limit. I expect they will have to double back a few times. Everybody is astonished at Dr. Freund not being interned. He is almost the only German at large in Sheffield.

Sandy Scott and his company left for France this morning. We had a short message. They don't expect to be in the fighting line till just after Christmas.

How are your hands, Mama? I've got some real bonnie hacks that make me sit up occasionally. We are back to biting cold weather. Better bring a lemonade bottle with you when you come.

We go to the University Musical Society concert tomorrow and must get into evening dress for it. Invitation too to the Boys' High School concert next Saturday - addressed to Mr. and Mrs. H.J.W.H. and family! Better lend us Alan[16].

Try not to worry, - I know I could cheer you up if I could be beside you. Had you a good time at Bearsden?

Love from all of us.

Your Ailie

I enjoy teaching the Belgians. Have had two lessons, - other two next week. If I can find time I shall try to take some more of them.

Chapter 3

"Your people suggest some quiet place in the Highlands. That will do all right. But I must ask that you do not visit Shettleston or its neighbourhood."

Duncan Cameron Mann, called Micky by his family, was born on 5th January 1915 at Jessie's aunt's house in Morningside in Edinburgh. Jessie's stay with her aunt was short-lived however as despite Hector Hetherington's advice, Jessie's family complied with Hugh's uncle's request that Jessie should not live in either Shettleston or Edinburgh and that their marriage should remain secret. In order therefore to provide Jessie and her son with a secure home Jessie's mother took the remarkable step of applying for a teaching post in Ardeonaig on Loch Tay despite not having been involved with teaching since her marriage nearly thirty years earlier. Her brave move appears all the more extraordinary in view of the fact that Jessie had a younger brother aged nine and sisters aged twelve and sixteen attending school in Glasgow.

The Schoolhouse in Ardeonaig, a tiny village on the south side of Loch Tay in Stirlingshire, becomes Jessie's home for the next few years. Her mother, Jessie Hunter Reid, takes charge of the nineteen pupil school in the peaceful and scenic village in early April 1915 while Jessie's father, brothers and sisters continue to live in their Shettleston home. The school and schoolhouse look across Loch Tay to Ben Lawers, a mountain which today is popular with hill walkers. Life for Jessie and her mother, accustomed as they were to the hustle and bustle of a large noisy city and a busy home where friends were always welcome, must have seemed very strange and isolated. In Jessie's time it would have taken the best part of a day to reach Ardeonaig from Glasgow. First there was the long train journey from Glasgow on the old Oban line to Killin Junction and then on the branch line to Killin. From Killin, access to Ardeonaig was by steamer. Visits from family members or friends must therefore have been rare.

Loch Tay and Ben Lawers

In 1986 when the number of children on the Ardeonaig school roll dropped to four, the small village school was closed. Today, the school building is in private ownership but sometimes used as a village hall and the schoolhouse is being refurbished. The three Loch Tay steamers which provided a link with the outside world are also long gone and access to Jessie's haven in the old schoolhouse at Ardeonaig is now by narrow road from either Kenmore to the east or Killin to the west.

Some letters written by Hugh to Jessie between January and June are missing, most likely lost by Jessie while in the throes of moving and looking after her young son.

On 15 January 1915 the 7th battalion of the Cameron Highlanders left Salamanca Barracks at Aldershot to march twenty miles to billets at Liphook. The men were at long last provided with regimental kilts although many had already bought their own uniforms. Equipment and appliances were still in short supply and there were only a few rifles available for the whole battalion. However substitute targets and dummy wooden machine-guns were soon devised by the men whose wealth of expertise from their former trades and professions was put to good use.

When the battalion left Liphook on 25 February for Cirencester, following an inspection by the French Minister of War, practically all the men were billeted in private houses. The men who were in excellent condition following their intensive training enjoyed their beautiful surroundings and the kindness of their hosts. The King's Head Hotel became the comfortable headquarters of the battalion and the men walked eight miles to and from their training area daily, sometimes returning in the evening for night operations. Once again tributes were paid to the "2000 Highlanders in the prime of manhood" whose "excellent behaviour and soldierly appearance" would never be forgotten.[17]

The battalion was on the move again on 6 April, this time to Chiseldon, a large hutted camp on Salisbury Plain. The men received training in musketry and on the 12 May they marched twenty-five miles with their full allocation of equipment to another camp at Parkhouse where some had to live under canvas. Lieutenant-Colonel Haig received a new appointment and was replaced on 22 April by Colonel J W Sandilands. When the brigade marched past Lord Kitchener on 15 May he described it as physically the finest he had yet seen. The King inspected the division on 21 June and finally, their training finished, the men received orders to cross the English Channel.

Loosley

Liphook

Wednesday

My dearest

Thanks for your last letter - a fine one. I am so glad that you and the prodigy are getting along nicely. I could not write to you before as I have had too much to do over our flitting. By the way, mother was suggesting that you should go somewhere near me, but I have replied saying that was impossible, as my movements are so uncertain. There was endless trouble over our flitting, and in the end we marched it - 15 miles with much kit on our backs + rifles - very, very heavy. Then here we are fixed in billets. I am at Coy Head Quarters - two empty houses. My room is with 4 other NCOs. It was the kitchen and we have a range of everything. Our attempts at cooking are rather amusing, but we have made it a rule to eat all we cook whatever happens, and the only result so far has been sore "stummicks". The place is pure country - very different and very much healthier than Aldershot. Discipline is of necessity a bit relaxed and there is a fine 'civvy' atmosphere, which is very refreshing. I have charge of two rooms on the very top storey, but it only means knocking them up at reveille, attending to meals and roll-call + lights out. I'm tired again to-night, so I'm going to close down. Good-night sweetheart.

Two kisses for you and the boy,

Yours,

Hugh

Loosley

Liphook

26th January 1915

My dear

I have not been able to snatch half a tick to write you, but Scott is away for his dinner, and I've a slack spell. We are pretty snug here in the meantime only there is not enough food. The countryside is very bonny, and in spite of heavy weather, I'm enjoying it fine. I was glad to hear that you and the prodigy are well. Now some business. It is my wish that when you are sufficiently strong and everything is safe, you should come south to some place where there is no danger of your being seen by old friends. Now in all arrangements that are made or are being made, remember that this is my unsentimentalised and sane view. This will probably be your bit of the sacrifice we are all making to put things straight, and I know that you will regard it so. If I were stationary, it might be possible to get near me, but of course as things are this is out of the question. You had best make a break for some big town; if it were me - London - but you will have to think round it, and get advice and so on. Here is my taskmaster back. Ring off.

Yours ever and only, H

ARDEONAIG *circa April 1915*

The Schoolhouse, Jessie's new home

Jessie and her young son, Duncan Cameron

Jessie's parents, William and Jessie Hunter Reid

Loosley

Liphook

Sunday

My dearest wife

I have been pushed for time, and also troubled about your situation - hence the delay in writing. Your letter was rather a *facer* to me, as when we spoke of such a scheme at Xmas, you didn't seem to dislike it so much. Now reading letters from you, from your mother and father and from my mother I seem to have all the threads in my hands. I have thought much of it and this is the general plan I propose for our future. Till the war is over, we must keep our counsel - (this talk of "facing things" is all very nice and pretty, and were we only concerned, we might do it - you and I have "faced things" together before, but for others' sake it is impossible. Let us not talk again of "facing things"). After the war we shall uproot and go to possibly Canada. There are many openings there where I can win my way to make an honourable home and position for you and ours - my chiefest concern and desire. That is the general plan I have in my mind, but this involves something for you to do - a line you have to pursue. I am trying to do my bit here, and I look to you confidently to do yours. You know what it is - merely to be inconspicuous. Well you evidently don't like England. Your people suggest some quiet place in the Highlands. That will do all right. But this I must ask - that you do not visit Shettleston or its neighbourhood. Write and say you will do this. Now I could write much more on this line, but I believe so much in your judgement and in your love that it isn't necessary. One thing - I received an extraordinary letter from your mother in which she talked of "persecution". I trust you do not share this view of mother's exertions on our behalf. She is spending her whole heart and soul and strength to help us - not herself, and for myself I feel that I can never repay her. Now, my girl, I want you to remember that behind all this detail of planning there runs a love between you and your boy, a love that nothing can break. I wish that we could talk it together and clouds would vanish; but whatever you doubt, never, never doubt my love. Take it all just now, and give what you can spare to our bairn.

Your husband

There is some difficulty about the way you are receiving money. Let me know how you want it and I will make arrangements.

Parkhouse Camp

Salisbury

1st June 1915

My darling wife

I have a nice little spell of leisure for a day as I am in charge of the Stable Guard - a plain job. There are practically no turn-outs and only one visit from the orderly officer, and for the rest it's a case of lying in a tent for twenty-four hours. I was quite glad of the rest, because we have been going thro' a good lot of hard graft these last weeks. We have been indulging in a form of amusement called Brigade Training, and only when you have got finished with that do you realise what real soldiering will be like. We had two days continuous operations last week. It meant being out from 4.30 a.m. on Tuesday till 3 p.m. the following day, covering over thirty miles in most fiendishly hot weather, skirmishing over miles of down, sleeping in trenches when it was a little more than cold, and getting practically no food. It was an interesting experience, tho' unfortunately my feet cracked up, and I finished on my toes. I believe we are finished with Brigade Training now, and next week we go on to a final physical course with heaps of bayonet fighting. We can't understand why we are still in this country for Kitchener inspected us a fortnight ago, and declared us to be the best and readiest brigade in the New Army. We hear tho' that all the new troops are to be delayed until the munitions are more adequate, as there is too great a wastage of men going on. This sounds quite probable.

I have been enjoying life fine since I joined the Sergeants' Mess. The food is ever so much better than in the men's mess, and there is more social life of an evening. It is somewhere to go when you are fed up. I hear that dear old Tim is much better, but that his ears are still discharging and he is still very deaf. Poor chap, he has had a very rotten time, and he'll take a bit of building up again. I hope all is right with you and baby. I haven't heard from you for a wee while, but I expect you find one Mann is enough to look after at a time. All my love, dearest.

Yours,

Hugh

> Camp
> Saturday

Dearie

Glorious news! By the grace of God I'll have three days in Scotland next week. I'm coming on to you first, and I expect to arrive on Friday night. Alas, it's short; for I'll have to leave Saturday night or early Sunday morning. Also I am liable to be recalled at (any) moment, as we are under orders - six hours - for anywhere on God's earth. I wish I didn't have to waste so much time in trains, but it can't be helped, and anyhow I'll SEE you again. Great, isn't it! This is scratchy again, old girl, but I guess you won't chip me this time. I'm Battalion Orderly which in the old-time vernacular is a "helofa" job.

All love and kisses that will soon be real. Ever your boy

Tell me how you get to your place.

2 London St
Edinburgh
Saturday

My darling

I got thro' all right, and to my intense relief discovered that my kit has arrived. So all is ready for the fray. I also received my railway warrant, and what do you think? I'm for the Northumberland Fusiliers! It's a good regiment, but I'm feeling as Arnold would if he were sent to the Camerons. However, mustn't grumble. There was one thing I meant to speak about. If you get for yourself a good map. I'll let you know where I am. Code thus. If a letter begins with a sentence of under six words, code is in the letter. Then the 2nd letter of the 3rd word in each succeeding sentence will be a key-letter. This will form the name of the place I'm at. When another sentence of less than six words comes, the code is off - got all that? Now when you do get information like that, it is for <u>you alone</u>. Absolutely confidential, *compris?* Well, cheerio, my well-beloved. Keep your own stout heart, and it will all come right. Back soon to make your dear life a burden.

Yours through all futures,

Hugh

Parkhouse Camp
Sunday

Dearest

What a stunning parcel I got yesterday and what a darling you are to send it. You haven't much to learn in the way of my peculiar tastes anyhow. Thank you very much dear. And now for the big news. Just 4 hours ago the wire came that we are to mobilize. The telegrams are all away recalling the furlough men. We are just hurling ourselves around to-day, trying to get things fixed up. All our kit is being sent to the depot at Inverness, and we only take what we can carry. We are supposed to leave on Wednesday for Folkestone and on Saturday or Sunday we cross to Boulogne. It is supposed to be because of the big massing of the Crown Prince army, and they reckon that it will want some stopping. We are as pleased as sandboys to get away, as this hanging about has been getting on my nerves. The address after about Saturday (unless I write otherwise) is 7th (Service) Battalion Cameron Highlanders, British Expeditionary Force, France. We are in a fearful hobble dearie, and I'm only snatching a little government time to write this. You'll understand. By the way, you may not get this till after we have moved. There is some word of stopping letters. In any case keep cheery. I'll write to you whenever the chance comes. But you won't have to get anxious if there are spells of silence. That's inevitable.

Finally dearest of all, God keep and guard you and our boy.

Your husband

PART III

France: July 1915 - October 1915

Loos 1915 taken from the booklet *Yuletide Greetings from the Cameron Highlanders - In the field Christmas 1918* sent to Jessie from the 5th Battalion.

The longest and the bloodiest battles of The First World War were fought by the allied forces against Germany on the Western Front. The trenched front which stretched 700 km from the Belgian coast to Switzerland altered very little in over four years of war and by the end of 1914 the conflict was already deadlocked. The British Expeditionary Force of regular and Territorial Army soldiers had suffered ninety per cent casualties in the early months of the war, most as a result of the First Battle of Ypres. Consequently the new volunteers of Kitchener's Army were shipped across to the continent as soon as they were trained. These eager young men took up positions on the stretch of the front line south of Ypres (Ieper) in Belgium. When Lloyd George became the new Minister of Munitions in 1915 the provision of war supplies improved considerably but, even so, an end to the war was nowhere in sight.

The Battle of Loos was one of the major battles on the Western Front in 1915. General Joffre, Commander of the French troops, planned a British attack against the German lines at Loos despite objections from Sir John French, the Commander in Chief of the British Expeditionary Force. The planned attack would have to take place across coalfields and a maze of miners' cottages. However, Kitchener, fearing that Joffre would be overthrown and that French politicians would make peace, ordered Sir John French to obey Joffre's directive. Because the British were to use gas for the first time, Haig, who was in charge in that quarter, was confident of victory. Unfortunately his optimism was ill-founded. British casualties were high: 15,800 dead and 34,580 gassed or wounded. The German fatalities were considerably lower with 5,000 dead and 14,500 gassed or wounded. Shortly afterwards Sir John French was replaced as Commander in Chief by General Haig.

Hugh, 1915

Chapter 1

"They are all women - scarcely a man in the village... They grab all our spare grub, and send most of it to Germany. Two of them have husbands there who have been prisoners since September, and they seldom have enough to eat."

Once Hugh set out to war he was subject to army censorship which stopped him disclosing his whereabouts or other details of military significance. Regimental records however provide a vivid backcloth for the letters and disclose that on 8 July 1915 the 7th Battalion of the Cameron Highlanders crossed to Le Havre from Southampton on ss Arundel. The men travelled by train to Houle where they billeted from the 10th - 15th before embarking on a three-day march to Houchin, arriving in darkness on the 18th as the village was only six miles from the firing line. New boots and paved roads caused much hardship to the novices. One of the first tasks for the men was to clear up the streets of Houchin. Lack of accommodation meant that seven hundred men had their first experience of sleeping under the stars that night. The following night the men moved on to Les Brebis as a detached battalion, the first of the 15th Division to enter the shelled area on the Western Front. Although shelling at Les Brebis was heavy, the novelty at first was such that the men would rush into the streets to see the effects of an explosion and to collect fragments as souvenirs. The companies then took it in turn to spend two days at a time in the trenches for instruction while attached to the 142nd Brigade of the 47th London Division. The men returned to Houchin on the 24th, some returning to trenches again for a further two days on the 30th. On 2 August the 7th Battalion took over the trenches for the first time at Maroc, holding the extreme right of the British line. On 10 August, when they were relieved by the 46th Brigade, they moved into billets at Mazingarbe, returning to the trenches on the 18th and taking over from the 6th Battalion of the Cameron Highlanders. On the 27th/28th the men returned to Mazingarbe but moved back to Noeux Les Mines on the 30th. They returned to the trenches on the 8 September before moving to billets at Verquin on the 13th. On the 21st the battalion moved to the Vermelles-Ornay branch line of trenches in preparation for the Battle of Loos.

Hugh was attached to D Company of the 7th Battalion. Regimental documents state that he is "to receive pay of rank (L/Sgt) dated 12/8/15". Although Hugh's letters indicate that his first spell in the trenches was short-lived as he was taken to one of the clearing hospitals, the official regimental records make no note of this.

France (somewhere)

Monday July 12th

Dearest Jess

"Here we are! Here we are! Here we are again!" We had a sudden notice to shift, as I expect all such notices are, and in no long time we are away, away - here. We are in a lovely little quiet village, billeted in a French farm-house. But it is not English billeting. There are about 40 of us in a barn, and the Army feeds us. Well, we rub along, and that's about the size of it. My feet have gone bad again, owing to the weight of pack. By the way, that parcel was more useful than perhaps you expected. I practically lived on it for two days. Correct and only proper address, "7th Cameron Highlanders, British Expeditionary Force, c/o GPO London".

Letters asked for,

Hugh

France

Tuesday, 20th July 1915

Dearest Jess

I have been writing at odd moments and making one letter do, asking mother to send 'em on to you - so you will have heard all about my wanderings up to being on guard in this new place. I came off late last night and found my billet. What do you think? Positively a bed - a funny one, but still a bed. I rolled into it and slept like a *deader*. And when I woke there was your parcel beside me. What a find! You have no idea how good everything in it is, and especially the Gold Flake. I was a whole week without cigs and it was pure torture. Thank you dear over and over again. The Germans have been treating us to high explosive shells all morning, and they do make a mess of things. It's really hardly worth while trying to keep the place tidy! They have been going for a church - of course! But I don't think they've got it yet. I hear that five children have been killed. None of their shells have come nearer my billet than about 400 yards. But the very first this morning burst just where my guard was yesterday. They make a fearful clatter, but unless you are within at least 100 yards, you are all right. Our boys were up last night digging reserve trenches, but were quite undisturbed. Some nights it is like a Sunday at home: others there are stan-shells and coal-boxes and all sorts of lively things. Well, dear, I'll get another wee sleep now as we'll likely be going up again to-night.

All love and again thanks that can't be written.

Ever yours,

Hugh

France

Tuesday 27th

Dearest Jess

I got a big parcel on Sunday with the mark of your delicate taste on its 'Contents'. One had a mighty good day after the post arrived. Everything was top-hole. I wonder if a little slab of butter would carry freshly. It would harmonise with the oatcakes like a Strauss Symphony.

We are still lazing around a fair piece behind the *point de feu*. By the way, I admire your nerve in chaffing my French. I am convinced that only the filthy patois stands between me and a complete understanding. My accent is excellent in the limited terms I permit myself to use, and you would scarcely know the difference between my pronunciation and that of a native in that treacherous little word *'Oui'*. Well, sufficient babblings for one letter.

Love to all,

Hugh

Postcard, front

Postcard, reverse

Hospital

France

August 7th

Dearest Jess

I've been having a few peaceful days in the middle of all the clatter in one of the clearing hospitals not far from the firing line. I was sorely smitten for many days with a painful diarrhoea, and was sent here to get sorted up. This has been done to a certain extent and I'm being sent back to duty to-night. I'm practically better, only weak, and I expect after a few days in that modern convalescent home - the first-line trenches - I'll be as fit as a fiddle. I got your last fine parcel and the biscuits kept me in life for 3 days when I could eat nothing else. I'm looking forward to harrying the rest when I go up. By the way, I'm not very keen on brawn - so, if you don't mind, little one, cut it out.

I found trench-life quite exciting. Logan and I shared a swagger little dug-out, full of all kinds of animal life. We had very little rifle-fire, and only a few trench-mortars to keep things from being an absolute Sunday-school. Before I came away my company had one real war casualty, and it was a fool one. A clever lad lit a cigarette at night right behind one of our sentries. Of course the poor sentry got it in the head. He's not very bad tho'. The worst of the trenches is that you are always on duty, and always chasing your tail for sleep. The Sergeants have to patrol constantly, so with only 3 in the platoon, you don't get much leisure. Still it's *la guerre!* We shan't get a real understanding of the Hades it can be till we've had an artillery bombardment and a bayonet charge. By the way, and as an incidental, do you think this damn war will ever end? We are all wondering what has happened to Warsaw (haven't seen a paper for 8 days) as we expect its capture will mean heavy fighting for us all on this front. I hope they manage to stick it out. I'm so glad to think that you all are having a decent time. One would require some such comforting compensation for all this hurly-burly.

Love and more love,

Hugh

Envelope

France

Friday 13th August

Dearest Jess

Thanks for two letters from you. Also another of your awful good parcels. Yes, sure I'll *blether* for a spell. I was tremendously taken with the little chap's effort in letter-writing. He's a remarkable writer for his age ain't he? I rather envy you that quiet retreat in these bustling days. We are back at a little village - as usual filthy and fly-infested and are supposed to be resting. But we are at physical drill every morning at 7.15 and most of the day we are working on the farms giving the natives a hand to get their stuff in. They aren't half-grateful, as well they might be, for they are very short of labour and a hundred able bodied *sojers* soon lick up a field. They pay us in beer - a very watery kind too, but still it's wet. One is pretty hot after 3 or 4 hours of forking, as the sun here is merciless.

I had a rotten thing the other day - a 43 hours' guard. I was shoved on on Monday night, and the battalion went away and left us on Tuesday night. We had to hang on till the incoming battalion relieved us, and as they were newly out and ignorant, they forgot about us till 3 o'clock on Wednesday afternoon. Had we not been decently treated by another lot we should have had neither breakfast nor dinner, as all the houses there were cleared three weeks ago. There were so many filthy spies. Two Germans were caught five miles on our side of the firing line, rigged up in Cameron kilts. Aren't they treacherous devils?

I did a good stroke of business this morning - pinched a new shirt from the Quartermaster. Saves washing the lousy one I had on in the trenches. I'm damn little use at washing tho' I'm real good at needle jobs. I've made down that shirt a treat: fits so well that I've to *dubbin* my shoulders to get into it. By the way those oatcakes and butter were ambrosial. They flowed in my interior for several days. I am almost better now of that wretched dysentery. The doctor said that if I hadn't been inoculated, I should have had typhoid, so that was a lucky escape anyhow. I don't know when we are leaving here - won't mind staying a long time. But just when you are shaping into a place, you've to shift. That's the *vie militaire* on active service.

Well cheero little lass,

Your boy

France

Wednesday 18th August 1915

Dearest Jess

Thanks for your letters and those dismal 'Heralds'. Things do seem a bit blue, don't they? There certainly doesn't appear to be an end for a good bit yet. In the part of the line where we are, both sides have stopped serious fighting for weeks, realizing that both defences are too strong for any attack to succeed. It's a proper stalemate. We are going back for a spell in the trenches to-day, but my Company are in reserve billets, so my luck is in again. Thanks also for the household p.c. I had been out on the long shift trench-digging - 7.30 p.m. to 2.30 a.m. and I found it when I got in. Tell Winnie that I am keeping my eyes open for wee blue devils, but this is a cheery crowd, and they are scarce. The only ones at all near wear spiked helmets, and they are a bit shy of being caught. If I nail one alive, I'll forward it. If unfortunately the life has departed, I'll send the remains on ice to any address in the United Kingdom.

I'm going about in fear of my life at this moment, as the two sections here have sworn to drink my blood. Reason? I kept them doubling with knees raised at physical drill till their shirts were round their necks. It's good for them to do a little graft sometimes. But it's no darned use telling them it hurts me more than them. The people here are very poor. They are all women - scarcely a man in the village. The folks we stay with keep a little *estaminet* and our boys have been shoving up their income. They grab all our spare grub, and send most of it to Germany. Two of them have husbands there who have been prisoners since September, and they seldom have enough to eat.

Well, the morning parade is just about due, and my buttons are still to shine. I'm on a special job to-night. All I know about it is - extract from orders: D Coy will detail a reliable NCO to take over 'Brigade Ammunition Store'. Well, I'm it. God knows why, but I'm always butting into jobs like that.

Love,

Hugh

France

1st September 1915

Dearest Jess

I am a little late this week with my scrawl owing to several rapid shifts, and guards extra. Also I have never had much new to say as, since we came down from our last spell in the trenches, it has been mostly routine work - night digging and *humphling* and carrying - all very necessary and important, but hardly exciting enough to be called "news". Indeed the most exciting thing we had was the arrival of your last parcel which was a winner. There was an awful lot of pleasure in getting thro' it. Also the 'Heralds' have been turning up regularly. They are pretty dismal reading, aren't they? The best of all are your letters when they come in. Silly of me to like them isn't it? But I do - some.

Hugh (centre of group). "These are some of the young gentlemen under my care. We have just come in from trenching, so we look a trifle tired. The room is in the back-ground. The window is of my bunk."

The weather has gone broke and we are having some chilly sleeps at night. We are usually shoved into barns, and many of them have fallen into disrepair. As there are holes in most of the roofs and doors, it is mighty draughty. I know not what it will be like in real winter - pretty bad, I fancy. This particular town is not bad in its way. Quite a lot doing in troops and so on. On a guard I was on two days ago we turned out and presented arms to the funeral of a French soldier. They are stereotyped, these things. First comes a man carrying a wooden cross, a slim white little thing, then another carries perhaps a wreath from the dead man's comrade - then comes the coffin in a quaint sort of cart. After that the officer, carrying his sword. Then a section of soldiers and at the rear a sorrowful woman or perhaps two clothed in black - his wife and mother. These funerals are unfortunately every day occurrences and attract little attention.

Well, I have really no chat. I'm going to get my leg dressed to-night. A damned mosquito bit it, and I knocked the top off. It's gone suppurated, and won't get better with my rude efforts. One's just as well to get fixed in decent order in case we go soon to the trenches.

Love to all,

Hugh

France

7th September 1915

Dearest Jess

Another 'Thank You' to the long list. Your last parcel was fine - I'm taking the "Lemco" up to the trenches when we go to-night, and with a little hot water it will be stunning at early morning 'stand-to'. We'll likely be in for eight days but one never knows in these hustling times. It has been a nice quiet spell down here, and we are about due some hurly-burly. The weather has not been good - rain, and cold at night. One can feel the beastly winter touch, a mild forecast of what is to come. I'm afraid it will be rather dismal out here when the winter really arrives. Let's hope the beastly war will be finished by that time. In these last few days, almost out of gun-sound, it has seemed almost as tho' there were no war. Only the eternal khaki and occasional aeroplane rémind you that you are not having your summer holidays. I was just thinking just now that I wouldn't mind being on holiday at a quiet little spot on a *Hielan'* loch. Do you think you could stick me for a month or so? I'll write you from *les tranchées* as there's *nix* doing here.

Love to all,

Hugh

France

19th September 1915

Dearest Jess

Thanks ever so much for the eggs, which were as fresh as paint. I suspect that there is a parcel of yours on the way, but for a variety of reasons the transport has been delayed. We are full of wars and rumours of wars here, so don't be surprised or worried if you don't hear for a while again. There may be nothing in it of course, but in any case emulate the Boy Scouts and be prepared. It has been all beer and skittles with us lately, so we are due a *towsy* spell.

This appears to be Sunday afternoon, and most of the humorists are snoring gently in the good old style, mouth full-cock, head well-back, elbows resting on someone else's chest - not hygienic but very satisfying. Only the flies are sleepless, *drat 'em!* There are two little kids paying me an afternoon call - curious big-eyed, flaxen-haired. They are like 18/11d dolls - the large size. The conversation is a bit one-sided. Either my French is worse than I thought it was or they are deaf-mutes. They will however in time make accomplished shop-lifters. The only thing they won't take is the only thing I can spare - my pack. They've just gone off - staggering and left the world to darkness and to me - did I already mention the flies? You will get a photo in a day or so - 'D' Coy sergeants.

The dog is a varlet attached to us for pay and rations. His name is the uncommon one of 'Jock'. His pay is like ours - barely visible to the naked eye. His rations are the crumbs that fall from our groaning table. We always swear that those army tables talk - the burden of their refrain being, "For God's sake put something on me fit for human consumption". Sorry I've no more green envelopes - like cognac and other heartsome things they are *"fini"* till *'après la guerre'*. Blethered enough for one afternoon.

Love,

Hugh

D Coy Sergeants. Hugh back right. Hugh sent this photograph to Jessie but a copy of it appeared in a Glasgow newspaper giving the following details.

"This photo, taken 'somewhere in France,' shows a group of the sergeants of D Company, 7th Cameron Highlanders. The names, reading from left to right are: *Back row* - Sergeant R. Anderson, Lance-Sergeant H.C.Winning, Sergeant W. White, Lance-Sergeant H. West, and Lance-Sergeant H.W. Mann; *Front Row* - Sergeant J. Girdwood Thom, Sergeant R. Gray, Company Sergeant-Major D. Adam (with "Jock" the mascot), Sergeant J.T. Page, and Sergeant R.S. Marshall."

Chapter 2

"I have lost nearly all my friends. I am the only sergeant left in D Coy, and the Coy numbers only fifty-four. But the Germans won't forget the 44th Brigade."

The 7th Battalion of the Cameron Highlanders took over the Grenay-Vermelles line of trenches on 21 September. News of the forthcoming attack had been kept secret from those below the rank of company commander. Nevertheless the Germans were expecting action and some of their soldiers, shouting across to the 7th Battalion's trenches, asked why their attack was being delayed.

Five battalions of the Cameron Highlanders were engaged in what has become known as the Battle of Loos on 25 September 1915, the first major battle for the 7th Battalion. The site of the battle was Loos-en-Gohelle, just north of Lens, not be confused with a larger town, Loos, south of Lille. One account of the battle in a history of the Cameron Highlanders describes the Battle of Loos as "one of the greatest in the history of Scotland, owing to the number of Scottish troops employed". The claim can be justified as the 15th Scottish Division, positioned just north of Loos, was comprised solely of Scottish Regiments. Furthermore, many other Scottish battalions formed part of other Divisions involved in the battle. It comes as no surprise therefore that a recent French book about the battle is dedicated, amongst others, "to the people of Scotland".

The book in question, *Loos-en-Gohelle dans la tourmente: Août 1914 – Août 1917* by Christophe Jupon, refers to the young men of the 6th and 7th battalions of the Cameron Highlanders as the "crème" of The University of Glasgow. It claims that they were killed not only because of their determination to uphold the courageous reputation of Scots on the battlefield but also to prove that they were *"autre chose que des cervaux"*!

.   The newspaper letter produced in this chapter describes the dramatic and destructive events of the attack on the 25th. It was published in the Glasgow Evening Times on 5 October 1915. It has not been possible to confirm that Hugh wrote it but it is very likely that he did considering a newspaper cutting featuring this letter had been stored with his letters. Because of censorship it is unlikely that he would have told Jessie of his intention to publish but his words in his letter of 29 September, "I expect you'll read about it in the papers some day," might have been a hint for her to be on the alert for his report.

The victory unfortunately was not as complete as the article makes out as the Germans retrieved some of the territory gained by the men of the 15th Scottish Division during the ongoing fighting on 26th/27th, but the devastated town of Loos-en-Gohelle remained free of German occupation for the rest of the war. The Germans recaptured the lower part of the eastern side of Hill 70, settling into their trenches about 240 metres from the summit. It was not until August 1917 that 12,000 Canadian infantry finally forced the Germans to retreat from the slopes of Hill 70. Sadly the victory was marred for the residents of Loos: German bombs once more razed their town to the ground.

Hugh's battalion suffered heavy losses during the battle for Loos and Hill 70 on 25 September. Immediately after the battle four officers were known to have died, four others were missing and six were wounded. Of rank and file soldiers sixty-four were killed, two hundred and seventeen were missing and two hundred and fifty-three were wounded. Other battalions also suffered huge losses with the total number of casualties from the 15th Scottish Division alone coming to over six and a half thousand men.

The 7th Battalion was ordered to withdraw to Mazingarbe on 27 September and on the 28th the men marched to billets at Houchin. As Sergeant R Gray who commanded Hugh's Company was wounded on the 25th, Hugh now took charge of the survivors.

Hugh's narrow escape must have made him realise how precarious his situation was: his will is dated 29 September 1915!

A view from Hill 70 towards the town of Loos 1998

France

29th September 1915

Dearest Jess

Here I am, but I don't quite know how. All I got was a bullet thro' my sleeve and a bit of shrapnel ripping my hose-top. Our battalion had a terrible smashing-up - 75% casualties. Shall I tell you the story? It's a good one and I expect you'll see it in the paper some day - the charge of the 44th Brigade.

We formed up in our own trenches the day before while a most terrific bombardment went on. At day-break we went over the parapet and at once men dropped. We got over the German line, but were held up 10 minutes at the barbed wire in front of Loos. We got it cut and went thro' into the town. What scenes! We were under heavy machine gunfire from the houses and each house had to be bombed. Then as we pushed them back, they came tumbling out with their hands up shouting "Camarade, friend". We rounded them up and sent an escort back with them and pushed on up Hill 70. We got to the top and away beyond, but our left flank had not come up, and so we had to fall back. The fire here was terrific and our own shrapnel was giving us fits. We took up position on the near crest of the hill and entrenched, or tried to, there, and at this spot we hung on till we were relieved at eleven that night. I never knew before what absolute physical exhaustion was. To add to our joy the rain was in torrents. Altogether hell can hold no hotter corner. For hours we held that damned line against constant counter attack, and ceaseless enfilade fire, and always one was waiting one's turn to be hit. It was horrible. Well, we came back and are now down a bit, and likely to go further for a rest. I have lost nearly all my friends. I am the only sergeant left in D Coy, and the Coy numbers only fifty-four. But the Germans won't forget the 44th Brigade. The Brigadier was seen in the base village with the tears running down his cheeks saying, "Glorious 44".

I will write more later dear. I'm responsible for the Coy just now, and also the fight has left its mark on me.

Love to all,

Hugh

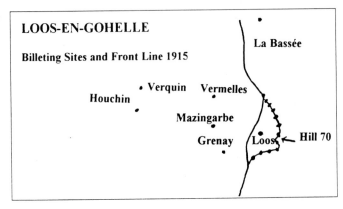

LOOS-EN-GOHELLE

Billeting Sites and Front Line 1915

La Bassée

• Verquin   Vermelles
Houchin

Mazingarbe

Grenay   Loos ← Hill 70

(The letter below appeared in the Glasgow Evening Times on the 5th October 1915.)

"WILL LIVE IN HISTORY." How the Camerons Fought.

THE WINNING OF HILL 70: Glasgow Man's Thrilling Story

A Glasgow man with the 7th Cameron Highlanders, writing on September 29 of the recent big fight, says:-

As you will probably have seen from the papers, the Allies have made an attack on a huge scale on the Western front, and I am sending you this letter to let you know how we are getting along.

For some time we have known about the attack, but it was only recently we got an idea when it was about to be made.

About a week ago, after being five days out of the trenches, we were marched back again. Previous to going in, the artillery had been heavily bombarding the German lines, but the night we arrived it commenced in real earnest and the din was something awful. It lasted for a few days, and on Friday night at eleven o'clock we were wakened and told breakfast would be at 3 am, Saturday morning. At that time we were dished out with same, but we had hardly commenced when we received orders to get on our equipment (less pack, which we had left in a village in the rear), and we commenced moving.

We were in the support trench, and we gradually moved down the communication trench towards the fire trench. The Germans, suspecting something, were heavily shelling us but fortunately the shells were falling short or too far, and we got to the fire trench without mishap.

When we arrived there our colonel was waiting for us, and gave us a few words of comfort, and then over the parapet we went. Part of our brigade was in front of us, and had got over the first line of German trenches, but we caught them up there. By this time the bullets were flying all roads. We captured the second line of the enemy trenches, leaving hundreds of Germans dead in them. Then commenced the worst part of the whole affair. The village of Loos was on our immediate front, and the Germans had been forced to retire there, where they were reinforced by their supports. We had about 1000 yards to go to reach the village. It was hellish. It was full of machine guns, and they sent over a terrible fire. My chums were dropping right and left, but we still kept on, only stopping at intervals for a breather. When we got to within 50 yards of the village their fire eased a bit, and what was left of us rushed ahead. It only took about half an hour to capture it. The Germans on the whole proved themselves cowards, as they would not face us. Those who did not retire threw down their arms and pleaded for mercy. We took hundreds of prisoners. That village was in an awful mess, mangled Germans lying everywhere. We had then to search the village, and in many of the cellars we found Germans chained to machine guns. It was too awful, but it was a glorious victory. We then set after the Germans, and forced them to retreat to Hill 70. After a terrible fight we captured it and pushed onwards. The Germans then took up a position in a village on the other side, where they received great reinforcements. As they were in houses and we had been greatly reduced in numbers, they forced us to retire about 200 yards to the crest of Hill 70. Our reinforcements met us there, and we held the enemy. We got dug in, and the enemy made terrible counter-attacks, but we never moved, and simply mowed them down. We then set to and established a position from which they will never shift us. We were then relieved and retired about four miles back to a village, where we rested.

Our Colonel has the D.S.O., but I think he will receive further honours, as he reorganised the whole line on Hill 70. Just before being relieved he said:- "There are many men here, as it is only natural that the regiments get mixed up, but I am speaking to the Camerons, and I have to tell you that what you have done to-day will live in history. You have lost heavily in numbers, but nothing like the Germans, and what is left of you I will do my best to take care of in the future."

There are two points I would like to mention, but before doing so I may say we have got the name of the "Shiney 7th," as our Colonel always likes us to keep our buttons, etc., clean and neat.

Well, the first point is:- The morning after we were relieved our Colonel told us to keep up our spirits, and tidy ourselves up. We all did so, and a few hours later we were paraded, and told we were going back to where we are now lying. We fell in and commenced to march back, and what was left of our pipers led the way. Just as we were leaving, the Brigadier-General rode up to see us, and as we marched past, sadly depleted in numbers, but, what was left of us, neat and tidy, the tears came to his eyes.

The second point is: - Our Colonel paraded us this morning, and read out to us congratulations from Sir Douglas Haig, etc., etc,, but he said there was one man more proud of us than any General, and that was our own C.O. (himself). I think he was going to say more, but he suddenly stopped and told us to dismiss, and as he walked off we saw he was drying his eyes.

In these few days we have made a great name for ourselves, even Regulars stop us and ask if we belong to the 7th Camerons, and when we say Yes, they congratulate us. The best of all happened to-day. Sir John French visited us and thanked us personally and said on behalf of our King he was proud of us.

We have suffered heavily, but we have gained a great victory. We have paved the way for the troops who follow us. We have driven the enemy out of trenches which he has occupied for months, and broken his lines completely. We have advanced further than any other part of the line. I know, too, that Hill 70 was our objective, and it was reckoned it would take us three days to reach there (if successful), and we managed it in 17 hours.

This is a hurried outline of what happened on our front, but it will never convey to you the real thing, as it is impossible for me to put on paper my feelings.

I am presently preparing for bed - at least I am going into my dug-out, which I have made in a bank in the field where we are staying. I believe we are going for a proper rest to some place in the rear.

The battalion's flag which was raised on Hill 70.

France
5th October 1915

Dearest Jess

I got a whacking big parcel from you to-day, and I wasn't half glad to see it, especially the cigs. Mother didn't send any, as she wasn't certain what had happened to me, but it was a bad point, for it left me without cigs. However, your dear little knock did the trick. We are well back now, and I am promoted full sergeant, so your allowance ought to go up some. I am also a platoon sergeant, and great glory! At the moment I am acting Coy Sergeant Major - great work, too, believe me. Reason - furloughs have started. Men are getting away, four at a time. I don't know when I'll get, but it should be within a month I fancy. Won't it be great? I'm not pinning my faith on it, but it ought to come off. By the way, cut out the bully beef, dear. We get it in great quantities here and we're a bit off it. Put in a John West's "Middle Cut" instead which is lovely. We are just beginning to realise our losses over that Loos and Hill 70 business. We had some fine things said to us and about us by all the generals from French downwards, but alas! That doesn't fill the gaps in the ranks. Well, dear, I'm in a hell of a hurry.

Best love, yours ever,

Hugh

À bientôt revoir Swank!!

The battalion's flag flying on Hill 70, a detail from *The Battle of Hill 70*, a painting by Joseph Gray, at The Regimental Museum, Fort George

PART IV

Inverness, Bristol and Invergordon: October 1915 - February 1917

The Inverness Militia at Camp, Cameron Barracks, Inverness, from a watercolour by Major R.A. Wymer, 3rd Camerons 1907

The beginning of 1916 heralded even greater loss of life and limb. The German offensive at Verdun continued from February to December 1916 with the loss of 362,000 French and nearly as many Germans. The British and French offensive on the Somme during the summer of 1916 sacrificed more than a million men in one of the bloodiest encounters of the war. British casualties were in excess of 400,000 with a loss to the French of 190,000 men and around 500,000 to the Germans. Despite such loss of life and some moves towards peace behind closed doors, decisions which could lead to an end to the war were as far away as ever. The war would continue for another two years even though, in the words of A J P Taylor, "Idealism perished on the Somme".

Kitchener's armies had raised a total of three million men. Nevertheless the enormous mortality rate made it necessary to introduce conscription in early 1916. Lord Kitchener himself, now powerless and no longer Secretary of State for War, was drowned on 5 June 1916 when the cruiser Hampshire was struck by a mine off the coast of Orkney.

Desolation

Chapter 1

"I got a great bundle from France, many asking about friends lost at Loos, and I want to reply to them all."

Hugh was still awaiting leave when, according to the battalion's "Daily Orders", he returned on 25 October to England "sick" on board HS Anglia. Although he expected to return to the Front from Folkestone, he appears instead to have returned to Scotland and not to have returned to France until early 1917. He was therefore fortunate in missing the Battle of the Somme where many more of his regimental companions were killed.

On his return he was involved for some time with the drafting of recruits. While at Inverness he appears to have had some contact again with the United Free Church. An extract from a sermon which is likely to have been written about this time has been included in this chapter. It is written on middle pages of an exercise book and numbered nine to twelve. Pages one to eight are missing.

York House

Cheriton Gardens

Folkestone

Saturday

Dearest Jess

Thanks for your letters. It is nice to get them so soon after they are written. It makes one feel not so horrid far away. Well, I'm still here, but just waiting orders to shift. When the next big convoy comes in I expect to get the order of the boot. I don't know where they will send me, but I'm so nearly fit again that I don't need to care. By the way you never tell me where Arnold is. I often wonder whether his battalion is still in this country or not. (Ink's run out!) Also is Howard still in Dunfermline? If he is, he must be fearfully sick of it. I'm getting pretty fed up with Folkestone. It's an awfully tame cat existence after the somewhat robust experiences of active service. This last may have its disadvantages in the shape of alarms and sudden deaths, but at least it is not dull. Now this is - decidedly so. You will scarcely believe when I tell you that I have been at a different picture-house every afternoon since last Saturday. Of course "wounded soldier" takes you anywhere free, and it's ten to one that some genial old maid stands you tea in exchange for which you buzz the tale. As a matter of fact you are compelled to lie like a Trojan. If you stick to facts and tell 'em that the trenches are as a rule all right, and that you get on an average three shells, and a couple of whiz-bangs *per diem,* they look at you as though you had done them over for a tea on false pretences. So you've to cram a week's shelling into a single day, and work the pip-squeaks into a hail-storm, chuck a few heads about, and work up the mangled remains, so that by the time you're sweating with French cakes they are sweating with reflected terror, and they are so busy over the size of the catastrophe that they never notice the size of the bill. The invariable question is, "And now, tell me, where were you wounded?" I always hedge them off this till I've had tea, for there's no romance in a crop of boils.

It is funny your getting that p.c. from Wimereux. The history of my various diagnoses runs something like this. Our own doctor - "Boils". First field station - "Farunculosis" - whatever the devil that is. Clearing hospital - "Bad boils". Rawal Pindi, Boulogne - "Scabies, slight". 14 General - "Scabies severe". 13 General - "Impetigo". So you can't quarrel about lack of definition. And you may choose whichever sounds most exciting. Myself, I'll have a tanner on farunculosis! I told them I think that the plain English of it was that I got badly bitten by several kinds of mosquitoes, that I got badly run down, and the bites all festered. The fatal and barbaric kilt!

Did you know that Jimmy Mackintosh was wounded at Loos and is now in a London Hospital? He is coming all right, but he got it pretty stiff.

I keep wondering what your latest comfort for your troops is to be. I'm not going to chance a guess tho' in case I get whiz-banged. Well, dearie, ta-ta-, I've blethered enough.

Love to all,

Hugh

2 London St

Edinburgh

15th December 1915

Darlingest, ownest wee wife

(That's better isn't it?) You're only going to get a wee scrap, as Tim is expected, and I've about a hundred letters to write. I got a great bundle from France, many asking about friends lost at Loos, and I want to reply to them all. But I want to break the good news to you. My railway warrant has come, and I'm to report at Inverness. Great happiness! It means a bit longer anyway. I had a great day yesterday. I was about drowned when I got to Killin. Had a glorious time with dada. We fell on each other's necks. Unluckily the pubs were shut. Saw the Jarvies. What good friends we've got, you and I, dearie. I'm going to buy a good torch-light with a bit of your X'mas present. It's very useful in France.

Dearie, you were kind, kind to me. It was just Heaven. My love to all, and the wee boy. Will you say a special 'Thank you' for me to Mama for all sorts of kindness that I can't put on paper. Best love, dear,

Ever your boy

Depot

Inverness

Monday

Dearest Jess

The pen is going to give place to the pencil, as to attempt to write much more with this one would mean insanity. First I hope you all got my timid attempts at X'mas presents. I'm not clever at things like that. Still they all go with my fondest love, and best wishes for a good time in the next year. I had quite a decent journey north, and found my old friends the Neils. Then I went up to the depot, and got a bed. The barracks are middling empty, and the place is very quiet compared with the bustling times of a year ago. There are a lot of "dug out" sergeants, and it is their pleasant custom to shove all the duties on the unfortunate blokes who are Expeditionary Force. Thus I was on canteen yesterday, and to-day I am depot orderly. To-morrow I'll likely be shoved on guard. Still I'm not grousing. It's a comfortable spot this. I saw the doctor on Saturday morning, and great happiness! - was marked for light duty. A lovely little boil showed up on my neck and I've encouraged its advances - so I may be here over X'mas after all. Good luck to it.

Is the wee *f'la* still keeping you awake at night? My darling, I did just love you when you were working with him. I hope he has the luck to have a wife like his dad's: but that's impossible. There's only one you, wee Jess. All my love sweetheart.

Ever your boy

Inverness

Saturday

Dear Jess

What a brick you are. I enjoyed your parcel immensely, and the biscuits are still on active service. It is still very quiet in here and I may be in for a few days yet. I'm really having a first rate time because these boils don't give me the least pain. It's an ideal malady for a person of my sunny disposition. What are you laughing at? We had a ripping concert in the ward last night at which the belles of Inverness warbled and wailed and gave us a good tea. *Très bon!*

Jessie and son at Ardeonaig circa January 1916

Then to-day I have permission to go out to tea at one of the wee nurses' house. She is sending up a cab for me!!! Poor delicate lad. She is young and impressionable, and not long at the job; also I have been spinning the tale about France to her until her eyes are starting from her head. Hence the tea and the cab. I doubt you'll say I'm getting very material, but indeed it is you who have pinched all the romance in me, and there is nothing left for other people but a healthy appetite to an ingenious imagination. Well, well. And how's the young *f'la?* Hope his complexion is back to the normal. It won't do to have him 'wee scabby-face', will it?

Love to Mama and you.

Hugh

Enter the butler - *loquit* - "My lord, the carriage waits!"

Inverness

(Envelope postmarked 28 June 1916)

Dearie

Yes, I have been down at Kincraig this week-end; hence the delay in your letter. Mr Morrison was so pressing that I didn't like to refuse, and off I went. I don't think I shall be down now for a long time though, as there is a man fixed up for the whole of July, and neither the boss nor I will be required.

On the whole I haven't done badly out of Kincraig, have I? Many a time it has been a welcome break from the monotony of barrack-life. This time it was quite decent, as the country was looking lovely. I had a drive of three miles for the morning service, and four for the evening. Now we are back at the old round, trying to catch the lead-swingers, and to lead in the proper path those who would fain dodge the column.

As you say the commission is well-nigh *fini*, and I'm thinking of asking to be returned to duty to have another spell overseas. This is all very well in its way, but it's a bit *tame-catty* while there is a war on. Also I feel perfectly fit and well, and able to stand any amount of battering about. I'm not doing anything though till I hear definitely that the commission is punctured, as if there is the slightest chance of training in this country I want to secure it.

I'm so sorry about your toothache. Don't you think it's high time you kicked everything up, and had them seen to? For goodness' sake, don't have false teeth. My best love, darling,

Yours ever,

Hugh

Extract from Sermon

You may have observed a growing tendency both in the press and in the pulpit to make light of the church, especially in its relation to our young men. It is said that we have lost the power to touch young hearts; that our message, once sharp as a sword, has lost its keenness. Criticism like this is as old as Saint Paul, and no man need be overborne in spirit because of it. One of the greatest Christians of all time said at the close of his strenuous day, "We have failed," and ten years later the Protestant revival swept Europe like a clean spring wind from the blue of heaven. Yet all criticism is worth considering, when the welfare of the church of God is at stake. Therefore let us ask our watchman of the church, "What of the night?"

We can obtain one or two inspiring suggestions from the experience of our chaplains on service, and these suggestions are stronger criticisms than spoken words; for they are the practical expression of our soldiers' thoughts and desires.

And the first of these is the impulse towards unity. Doubtless the circumstances under which services are held in France tend to obliterate sect distinctions, yet it is impossible to deny that differences are unpopular, and unintelligible. The curious thing is that just where there is most need of the church, just where Christ himself would minister, there, in full fellowship and harmony, are Catholic priest and Scotch chaplain. Men whose peril is ever-present reek little of Presbyterian and Church of England. They need Christ and him crucified, for is not theirs the daily crucifixion? It is only at home, when ease and security do their deadly, numbing work, that Christ His body is divided by men upon whom His gentle benediction has fallen. Read we the lesson! Every one of you saith, I am of Paul; and I of Apollos; and I of Cephas; I am Presbyterian; I am Baptist; I am

Church of England - Is Christ divided? Were you baptised in the name of the Church of Scotland - or in the name of the Lord Jesus Christ, the son of the living God?

There is a further and not less true criticism directed against the formality of our worship, which speedily translates itself into a formality of soul - when the last state of that church is desolate indeed. When sin enters the church there is hope - for there is One who casteth out devils. But when worship of the form is all in all, then that church is dead. It is like the cottage, wrecked by the ravage of war. There once the labourer lived with his family, and the warm fire flickered on the hearth at the close of day, and bright faces and happy voices rang the Evensong of praise. And now it is four grey broken walls. The life has gone. There is but death and memory. Can this not be truly said of some of our churches? Where our fathers brought their souls, their doubts, their sins, their fears, we bring cold hearts that are determined to do the correct thing at whatever inconvenience to ourselves.

Think you not that God sends his strong arm in the war-cloud to bring to us the real things of life - to teach us those elementary things that are so elementary that we forget them, and yet so necessary that without them we are lost souls. Ah! There are those who have seen God's face in the blinding shock of war who would never have raised their eyes to the calm skies of peace. There are those who in their sorrow have seen the Christ of Golgotha, who would never have seen Him on the Mount of Olives. Shall not the Angel of the Lord come to our churches, and rouse them - ay, if need be with a sword - to see the Anointed One of Israel, before whom every knee shall bow.

One cannot escape from the conviction that the strength of the church depends upon the sacrifice of its members, that if it is to be truly living, it must be caught up by the warm fresh life of consecrated souls. Yes, the night is dark; so was it when Paul upheld the infant church amid the crashing ruin of the Roman Empire; so was it when the saints of the Middle Ages tended its clinging life among savage men, who, having eyes, saw not; so was it when the strong-souled Protestants nurtured it to manhood amid the bitter strife of kings and captains; so was it when the Covenanters met on the grey hills when all men persecuted them. And so is it this day, when the harsh deeds of men burden the heart of the Christ, and the spoiler goes openly. The church of God will live in the sacrifice of the sons of God. What of the night? The night will pass, and joy and hope awaken, and the dawn at last shall rise.

2 London St
Edinburgh
Monday

Sweetheart

Pray excuse me for springing little surprises on you after this fashion. I was warned late on Friday night that I was to conduct a draft to France on Saturday morning, and I hadn't time to let you know. I've delivered my draft, and wired for three days leave, so that's all right. I'll be thro' to-morrow, but must leave the same night, as I want to go out to see Tim the following day, and I'm due back by Thursday night train. Tim hasn't been well lately, poor old chap, and it will cheer him up if I go. Well, till dear old tomorrow, darling.

Yours ever,

Hugh

Inverness
Sunday

My darling

You will be very anxious unless you have heard more of Arnold. He must have been in the big scrap. I do hope he has got just a sufficiently cushy one to bring him back to *Blighty* for a spell. Please let me hear from you whenever you get word. I hope the dentist didn't give you too much *'gyp'*, and that you have your teeth all fixed up *good-o* now. You would enjoy your trip to Glasgow. Tell me, were you glad to get back to your quiet spot again, and do you prefer country to town?

I hope you managed to see Mrs Jarvie. I'm going to write to her to-day if I manage to get time.

I was just recalling that a year ago this morning we set foot in France, and were lying in a damned lousy rest camp on the hill at Boulogne. I can smell the place yet.

Well, the work is slacking off here, and I shouldn't wonder if we get the sack soon. Shan't be sorry, girl, for I'll get a few days' pass.

I had a letter from Mr Inch of Dumbarton in reply to a letter of sympathy of mine. Poor John, I'm awfully sorry about it.

Well, *ta-ta*, dearie. Yours ever,

Hugh

Depot

Sunday

Darling

I know you will have *cussed* me for not writing, but I couldn't help it. We've had a furiously busy spell, and as I had hellish indigestion some time back, I shove all the exercise I can into the non-working hours.

Apart from the crowd of men we have had to deal with, there has not been much exciting happening. Still no word of commission, and still no word of shifting. So there we are. My bunk-chum Smithy, however, has got his *chuck*. He left yesterday for Invergordon. When I came into the bunk late last night, here was a hairy specimen of a sergeant in Smithy's bed. He was so damned drunk that I couldn't waken him to ask him what the hell he wanted. This morning he waked me up at six to chat about Salonica, and for two stricken hours he babbled away. If there is one spell of peace I love more than another, it is from six to eight on Sunday morning. I didn't half strafe him.

He turns out to be a 2nd Battalion man sent home with hernia. I don't think he'll stay long in my bunk anyhow. I'm going to get an old hard-necked Irishman in with me - Stoole by name. He is an ancient *dug-up,* and full of devilry, but decent withal.

I'm just fair longing to see you and our nipper, and if something doesn't turn up soon, I'll desert. I take spells of desperate longing to see you, Jess, and hold you in my arms, and kiss you till you cry for mercy. Good God, here is the ancient married man making violent love to his wife like a love-lorn swain. I do love you, Kiddie, and I apologize for blethering about it, but sometimes I fair can't help it. Cheerie-o, littlest one.

Ever and ever your Hugh

Write and tell me you love me.

Inverness

Monday

Dearie

The boss has been away at Kincraig, and I had a quiet week-end on my own. He has not returned yet: hence this neglect of Government interest for my own. The weather has been absolutely top-hole, and I've had a good time. On Saturday I had twelve sets of tennis between two and ten. Great sport, and all hot matches. I'm getting much better now, and I wouldn't be scared to tackle you single-handed. Then on Sunday I worked in the morning, and went round to Neil's in the afternoon. Read a whole novel by supper-time, and went for a spin on Morrison's bike after supper. No wind, and a perfect road together with a three-speed gear made it a rare pleasure. And this morning we are back to the old routine.

The boss is expecting to bring his sister and his fiancée up to Inverness to-day, so I expect I'll have to take them to the pictures to-night. I guess I'd rather be golfing in weather like this, but Morrison has been the prince of good fellows so far as I am concerned, and I'd do a lot to oblige him.

It must be lovely at your place just now; I wish we could have it together even for a day. How slow that wretched commission is! I am beginning to despair of it ever coming through. What do you think? My love, darling.

Ever yours,

Hugh

Schoolhouse at Ardeonaig with Ben Lawers in the background.

Chapter 2

"And how I wish this darn war was over."

Hugh left Inverness in mid or late July to join the Cadet School in Bristol. On the 25 October 1916 he was gazetted 2nd Lieutenant and returned to Scotland shortly afterwards. While in Bristol Hugh joined Jessie for some days in Cardiff where Jessie's sister Alison and her husband Hector were now living.

It is not known at what point Hugh and Jessie's marriage and the birth of their son became generally known. Jessie continues to live in Ardeonaig but some letters from the summer of 1916 are addressed to Jessie at her family home in Shettleston.

Cadet H Mann 13902

C Coy

No 3 Officer Cadet Battalion

Queen's Hotel

Bristol

Thursday night

Dearest Jess

A bad pencil, but I'll begin to-night. This is a fine place - a big hotel - empty rooms with trestles and straw palliasses. There are from 600 to 700 cadets, and I've struck me on two decent chaps already.

I had a hell of a journey down last night and to-day - a slow train right across England. To-day has been fearfully hot, and I don't know what parades will be like. But it looks as though the months will be very pleasant. Tim's address will be 4 Roxburgh Terrace, Dunbar. I'm going to sleep now, dearie. Would I were back with you.

The following morning, and a damned hot one. This place is revelling in a heat wave at present, and it's almost impossible to breathe without sweating. We have been issued with white bands and full equipment. The white band on the Glengarry looks rotten. Thank God it's not for always. One is treated very well here. Feeding is quite good. The dining-hall is the main speech room of Bristol University College. There are eight fellows in my room, and I'm the only Jock. All kinds of regiments seem to be here - English, Irish, Welsh, Canadian. We have done no parades yet, but there was a kit inspection this morning by a very humorous captain who is our O.C. Coy. Week-ends will be fairly frequent - 20% of the Coy from after duty Saturday to midnight Sunday. We have had to take our stripes down, and are now cadets.

The dinner is just about due, so I'll close up; dearie it was fine even that little time with you, my own wife, and I wish the darn war was finished ---. Love darling.

Yours,

Hugh

No 3 Officer Cadet Battalion

Bristol

Monday 14th August 1916

Dearest Jess

We have had a nice quiet week-end, but as usual very hot. This blinking climate gives your kid the pip. It's impossible either to work or to enjoy yourself without sweating buckets all the time. On Saturday we had the usual inspection of quarters: in the afternoon we all lay down upon our boards, and forgot about three hours. Then after tea we went knocking round the streets, and for a good walk, which was the only evening last week I was out of the hotel. I'm pretty rusty, and I've had to swot every night to pull things together again. It's damned monotonous, but it's coming back slowly. Anyhow I'm not going to get spun on my exams, if I can help it. It took too much doing to get here to fall down on it now, didn't it, old lady?

Yesterday morning, Sunday, I was at the Presbyterian church. There are only about a dozen of us, so no one can dodge it. We trail about two miles to a kirk that usually contains three men, five women and a kid or so. The parson's face is like a sheep's, and his sermons do not convince one that his brain is much of an advance on the same *animile*.

In the afternoon, I called on Mr and Mrs Taylor - the married sister of Miss Munro in Inverness. They stay in a charming house in the swank end of the town. We had a topping tea in the garden, and in the evening Taylor and I went for a walk. About nine we dropped into Taylor's brother's house, another high-brow shop, and had supper. They are very kind people, and I'm to go golfing with them, and am also asked to lunch in their club. It should be a decent break between parades.

To-morrow afternoon the whole company is marched down for its weekly wash to the Corporation baths. Don't run away with the idea that this is the only scrape one has. There are fine baths in the hotel, and personally I have a cold one every morning at 5.30 a.m., and usually one later in the day after parades. But this is - God knows why - on the supposition that we are not all thirsting after cleanliness.

When we were there last week the place was full of small boys from the lower quarter of the town. Consequently if you happened to dive unwarily, you hit not water but boy. It wasn't pleasant to excess, but perhaps it will be better this time.

One of our chaps was thro' at Cardiff this week-end. He went with the 12 train on Saturday, and left Cardiff at 10 something p.m. on Sunday night. So that's all right. The only thing is that there is rather more than a chance of leave being stopped owing to this infernal epidemic. It turns out to be bubonic plague, and the Government has sent down some 200 rat-catchers. Damnable, isn't it? However it may be got rid of before you come along. In any case, dear, let me know a good few days in advance, as it takes a day or two here to get one's pass thro'. Do you think Hector and Alison will mind the general invasion?

This has turned out a long and most uninteresting epistle, and the apology in two heads: (1) that you complained once or even oftener, of the scanty letters I sent you; (2) that I've just finished swotting King's Rules and Regulations, a very dry subject, and am going on to Field Service Regulations which is damn little better. Am I forgiven? Ta-ta, bonnie wee sweetheart, and to our soon meeting,

Ever your boy

> No 3 Officer Cadet Battalion
>
> Bristol
>
> Friday

My darling

Just been thro' a very stiff medical exam, and I didn't half get a roasting over my wretched eye-sight. The chap didn't say anything at the end of it, so I'm hoping I'm through. Anyhow it's over, and that's always some suspense removed.

Still enjoying life here. The work is hard, especially as I've been so long away from it, but one is treated with all sorts of consideration both by officers and NCOs. I haven't been out much at nights as there's a lot of book-work to get over. Indeed it's quite like old times taking down lectures, and casting notes. I'm afraid I'm dreadfully rusty in the whole process.

Half of the town has been put out of bounds for the troops owing to an outbreak of cerebro-spinal meningitis, and the Railway Station is included in this half. I'm wondering if it will affect week-end leave. Hope not; anyway I'm glad you're not coming down just for a bit. It will give things time to clear up. I don't appreciate much that long journey of yours alone, especially as so many queer characters in and out of uniform are travelling. If I were you I should come down thro' the day, arriving not too late at night, and travel in a compartment with women. Avoid talking to strangers. Pardon all this paternal advice, but I'm a bit anxious for your dear safety.

Well, got to get out on parade now. Heaps of love, dear one.

Yours

Hugh

Bristol

Wednesday night

Dearest Jess

Here's more trouble. There is a damn General coming to inspect on Saturday, and we have been warned that we may not get away till 2 o'clock. So I'll just have to get through when I can. There is also a War Office letter suggesting that only one leave be given in the middle of the course. But I don't think that will stop this week-end.

Hope you got thro' comfortably dearie. It's night, and I'm missing you horribly.

Love to all,

Hugh

Bristol

Wednesday

Belovedest

Night, and a damned wet one too. Since Sunday the weather has been broken, and it looks as though we were in for a spell of it. I can see that this place is going to be very dull in winter, and I don't think I shall shed many tears when my time is up. Apart from anything else, I have the memories of your visit to me, and I can't deny that things have been a bit flat since then. Still and on, what a grateful heart I have that you could come, and that you were so good to me. My dear, you are more than anything one can mean by 'wife'. You are the truest pal ever a man had. Sometimes I think Jess, love such as ours is more than £.s.d. We certainly haven't much of the latter commodity, but somehow I think we'll win through in the long run.

I hope you got up safely and with comfort. Give my best love to papa and Win and the others. I've been in all night partly to work, and partly because I'm broke till Friday. I'm going in for a scheme of compulsory retrenchment which is very good for the soul, but hellish for the temper. Let's hear from you soon, darling. Ever yours,

Hugh

Cold still pretty heavy.

Bristol

Sunday

Sweetheart

I got your dear letter from Shettleston, and I was quite surprised to hear that you still loved me. You are a little darling, but hard to manage. Yes thanks, I got that poke in the ribs.

I have had exactly one hour to spare this morning thanks to the change in the time, and my own failure to appreciate it until it was too late to slumber longer. A sad business!

Well, there is nothing new on here. D Company have gone through their final exam, and are away to begin afresh the great adventure. It will be our turn quite soon - in fact the sooner it comes the better I shall be pleased, because you know what it means, don't you? We shall have another dear little spell together, girl, and won't we be happy again.

It's got quite chilly here now and I prefer it, as it makes parades and work generally much easier. I still have a bit of cold knocking around, but I'm hating it with eucalyptus, and it's going 'to die' shortly.

Let me know how Arnold is and what his plans are to be. I do hope he wangles an extension from that medical board. It used to be easy to manage, but I don't know about it now. I expect things are tighter all round. Well, write soon again, dearie.

Yours,

Hugh

Hugh, third from left, back row. "Bristol 12.10.16. Con Amore."

Chapter 3

"I have asked, and been allowed, to attach myself to the Machine Gun lot here."

Hugh, as 2nd Lieutenant, returned to Scotland where he joined the 3rd Battalion of Cameron Highlanders at Invergodon, north of Inverness on the Cromarty Firth. The 3rd Battalion was a special reserve battalion made up of men awaiting draft. Although the first letter from Invergordon is dated 3 December, Hugh must have been stationed with the reserve battalion for some time as records for the 16 November indicate that he is due leave from 18 - 24 November.

> 3rd QO Cameron Highlanders
>
> Invergordon
>
> 3rd December 1916

Dearest Jess

Here is another bonnie Sunday, and I am still without warning for abroad. There have been large drafts of men however and I expect officers will be required presently. The time has been passing much as usual, and what with parades and meals it soon flies. It has been bitterly cold lately, and most of our faces are skinned with the *ber-last*. I'm waiting now for the mess-bill which should be coming along to-day or to-morrow. I think a fiver will hold it.

Thank Arnold for his postcard. I'm jolly glad his board has not materialised. The longer it takes, I guess, the better he will be pleased.

And how are you, *mon ami?* Still enjoying the town? Tell me how Mamma is getting on in Ardeonaig. I often think of her in this weather.

Well, dearie, there isn't anything happening here worth recording, so rather than blether, I'll shut down. All my love to you both.

Yours,

Hugh

> 2 London St
>
> Edinburgh
>
> Saturday

Dearest

Just got down this morning, and owing to damned order re no troops to travel between 22nd and 26th I have to return on Thursday night. I am really down to interview the dentist, so I won't get to you till Tuesday, and I'll have to return Wednesday. I've just wired you, as you didn't mention how long you were to be in Ardeonaig. I don't want to arrive there to find that you are in Shettleston.

See you soon, soon, girl. In haste. Yours,

Hugh

Invergordon

23 December 1916

Dearest Jess

I reckon you should get this on Christmas morning, so here's wishing you a mighty merry one; also to all the family assembled. I expect unless there has been a big thaw, it will be a *gey* snowy one. Up here there has been no snow at all, but any amount of frost. It is quite an amusing sight seeing a battalion slithering all over the place. My young pal Macleod returned a salute to-day from a sitting position, when his heels had abandoned the effort to support him.

Well, I got along on Tuesday, but it was very hard walking, and I was *gey* *"wabbit"* when Killin hove in sight. I tried to avoid the painter's; but they caught me, and hauled me in to an excellent dinner. They are most decent people. I was telling Mrs Bickerton that Mamma had had some difficulty in getting certain supplies, and she says she is just to let her know, and she will get anything quite easily.

Mother was better when I got back, but rather groggy. Everyone wants to write letters to-night, and I am being urgently requested to cut it short. Well, dearie, I was glad to see you looking so well, and the boy too. Hope to see you again soon.

Write soon. I was expecting a letter to-day. All my love.

Yours ever,

Hugh

Did Papa get the canary safely up?

3rd Q.O. Cameron Highlanders

Invergordon

24th December 1916

Dearest Jess

I've just come in from that weary affair - church parade. In this place it involves a tramp of over a mile through sloppy woods and turnip fields, with a monotonous parson at the end of it. So you can understand what a pleasure it is to get it over for another week.

I'm sorry I forgot to say how nice the wee photo was. I like it real well. You might let me know if Arnold is marked 'fit' by this board. I do hope he will get another month to put the worst of the winter past. I had a long letter from Nancy

Jarvie telling me that you had been in with the sonnie boy. Nancy was saying she had not been so well. Rotten, isn't it? Well, the mess-bill came in, and turned out to be £2-16-10 for half the month. That's not too expensive, is it? I had been trying to get a wee leave at X'mas, but I'm shoved on a Bayonet Fighting Course this week so meantime it's in abeyance, but I may manage down yet for a day or two. Then we can have one of our own glorious times, can't we, dearie?

Here's lunch now, and if one doesn't go in at once, greedy pigs devour the hot dishes, and one is left with cold. So I will *avaunt*. All my love, sweetheart.

Yours,

Hugh

Father and son circa December 1916

Invergordon

29th December 1916

My darling Jess

Thanks so much for your good long letter, which I got this morning. Glad the youth is in such sparkling form. It will make your days merrier. I was just needing a nice tonic at the time, for an unhappy incident occurred in which I occupied a small part of the play.

Last night there was a lecture by one Lochiel on 'The Battle of Loos'. As attendance was not billed as compulsory, about sixty or us stayed away and we all received an invitation to meet the Mackintosh at orderly room this morning couched in such urgent terms that we could hardly decline it. A very one-sided interview occurred, and as a result all our leave was stopped for this week-end at least. I had arranged to go to the Munros, and eat my New Year dinner, and behold I must stay my hunger in Invergordon or go empty. This has fed one up rather, but it can't be helped.

I'm very glad to hear about Howard, and that he is getting on all right. Well, I'm sorry to inform you, old lady, that mother is in bed again with a recurrence of asthma and bronchitis, and in addition some digestive trouble arising from it. It is very abominable, and also not a little alarming, as her strength, which is never great, has been undermined by the first attack.

Altogether it's not a great New Year, but let me wish for you that it may be bright as your dear eyes, and bring you the love you long for.

Ever yours,

Hugh

3rd Q.O. Cameron Highlanders

Invergordon

11th January 1917

Dear Lass

You have been very patient with my *press des affaires*, which has been moderately "some". The bombing course last week was a case of notes during the day, and much writing up till late at night. I needn't have put so much work into it, but I got interested.

I suppose by this time, old sweetheart, you are back in Shettleston. Gee, I would like to share a week or so with you, but we are tied up tighter than ever. Not only is Invergordon still out of bounds, but Inverness in addition, and to crown the lovely lot there came a letter from Scottish Command that all leave must henceforth be cut down, and only urgent things could carry weight. Don't you wish the war were over, and you and I were finished with this cursed "Thou shall" and "Thou shalt not"? I guess I've got the hump to-night old lady. So write me one of your darling letters just brimful of your dear self. I sometimes get fair wild for you, girl. But I suppose one mustn't grouse. All my love, precious.

Yours,

Hugh

Invergordon
23rd January 1917

My dear

Here we are settled down again in the old way, just as though there had been no lightning interview with the little woman. And yet not quite the same, is it? For I rather think we are both heartened by each other, and fit to go another spell. It may be no long time before we manage another little break. Everything up here is as per usual, and a few new faces always coming in, and some old ones clearing out for various reasons, but still no word to move over the sea. I have asked, and been allowed to attach myself to the Machine Gun lot here, partly to fill in the time a trifle more interestingly, and partly to learn the Lewis Gun. One never knows when knowledge will be more than useful.

Your dear parcel was intact, and waiting for me. There was nothing spoiled about it, and I enjoyed the contents fine. You are a darling lassie and awful good to your boy. My pal Hay is away on leave for a few days, and I was just thinking I might have you sharing it. Alas, in this bachelor camp, it would hardly do. We are once more confined to camp owing to numerous cases of measles. Even when we want a walk we have to sneak out by the woods. It's damnable. I hope the mischief-maker is behaving himself these days. One does miss you both. However, *courage, mon amie,* and by the by *le diable sera mort.* All my love, love-lass.

Yours,

Hugh

3rd Q.O. Cameron Highlanders
28th

Dearest Jess

The Sunday Chronicle! On the West, East, and South lines there is nothing to report. Our own Northern front, the Cromarty Defences, continues to be strengthened by the presence of 2/Lt H W Mann. This distinguished officer had a conference with the GOC on the best method of evading work. It is understood that the General was much impressed by the novel and effective methods used. It is now certain that victory will be ours. *AAA.*

Well, lass, I've been doing little to-day but shoot. There has arrived at the camp a stalwart youth from Driscoll's Horse, who has been in most odd corners of the universe. He is a marvellous revolver shot, and has been giving me some tips in shooting. It's great sport when you get on a bit.

I had a mishap the other day which may give me a little holiday again. I managed to smash my crown tooth. The Adjutant wanted to give me three days' leave, but as that would likely prevent me from getting thro' to you, I stuck out for seven. I don't know yet whether I'll get it or not. In any case we may be away before anything comes off. Hay, my pal and four others left for France yesterday. They will have two days at home, so I'm sure of seeing you in any case before I go out. For the rest there is the usual nothing doing, and life is moving slowly. I would have given a lot to have got off with Hay. He was a nice chap, and I was very fond of him. All my love, dearest, and here's to a little visit soon.

Yours,

Hugh

PART V

Arras: February 1917 - August 1917

Arras, April 9th 1917 from *Yuletide Greetings from the Cameron Highlanders* sent to Jessie, Christmas 1918

When Lloyd George became Prime Minister in December 1916 he aimed to move the main arena of the war from the Western Front to the Italian Front. Nevertheless the major offensives continued to be on the Western Front as the Allied Conference in Rome did not approve of the proposed change. Because Lloyd George had no faith in Field Marshall Sir Douglas Haig, the Commander-in-Chief of the British Forces in France, Haig was forced to cooperate with General Robert Nivelle, Joffre's successor as Commander-in-Chief of the French Forces. Despite widespread objection, Nivelle chose Arras for an allied offensive, the Battle of Arras taking place between 9 April and 5 May. With the exception of the Canadian success on Vimy Ridge, the offensive proved to be another major disaster resulting in 150,000 British and 100,000 German casualties. The French infantry also suffered huge losses and many divisions reached breaking point. French soldiers deserted in their thousands and Nivelle, whose command was leading to a mutiny of French troops, was quickly replaced by General Pétain. Haig on the other hand, who had the support of King George V, retained his command until the end of the war.

As the front-line ran just east of Arras, the city was badly destroyed by enemy bombardment between 1914 and 1918. Civilians and British troops lived in chalk caverns and tunnels under Arras throughout the war, often deafened by the noise of shelling devastating the city above them. The Germans were unaware at the time of the existence of the tunnels, some of which had been built in Roman times. The troops based in the tunnels would not surface until they had completed a six-month stint. Many were involved in building more tunnels stretching out to 'no man's land' between the allied and German trenches.

June 1917 saw the first soldiers of the American Expeditionary Force under General John Pershing arrive in Europe. The Americans, although openly siding with the Allies, had not wanted to become involved in the fighting but the sinking of American ships by German submarines and a German prank relating to New Mexico forced them to declare war on Germany. Despite their involvement it would be some time before the Americans would have sufficient soldiers trained to alter significantly the course of the war.

Chapter 1

"The usual leave crowd on the boat, and plenty much chop in the channel, then jolly old France again. It is as mucky a hole as ever, only more so."

On returning to France in February 1917 Hugh Wallace Mann was assigned to the 5th Battalion of the Cameron Highlanders which was attached to the 9th Scottish Division. In December 1916 the battalion had moved to Arras to take up positions near the River Scarpe. Hugh joined the battalion which was billetted at Ostraville but marched to Hermaville on 2 March and then closer to the front line east of Arras to billets known as Y Huts. The situation was relatively quiet at first although on the 6th aeroplanes were very active and there was heavy shelling near the Candle Factory. When the battalion moved into the trenches five were killed and two wounded on the 12th and 13th. Hugh's Company, D Company, moved to Forestier Kidoubt and the Candle Factory on the 21st and spent the 22nd digging assembly trenches. On the 24th they were relieved by the 8th Black Watch and moved to the Brigade Headquarters in Arras. On the 29th the battalion moved back to billets in Hermaville in preparation for another spell in the trenches and their first attack of the Battle of Arras.

NO 19 1BD
APOS 17
BEF
France

Dearest Jess

Here we are again! I have been travelling one way and another the whole time since I left Shettleston, and behold I have found a resting-place at last. I won't attempt to describe all the ins and outs, mostly of trains. We had bad luck(!) in missing the boat-train from Victoria on Monday morning, and got the day in London. So we approved of the bad luck in the end and made quite a good thing out of it. It was all we could do to catch the following morning's train, but by the grace of God we managed it. The usual leave crowd on the boat, and plenty much chop in the channel, then jolly old France again. It is as mucky a hole as ever, only more so. Roll on peace! We are under canvas here, and it's mighty cold. They say they are having the coldest weather they've had in France for 40 years. Anyhow, it's cold enough for me. Give my love to all old lady, and heaps to yourself.

Yours,
Hugh

Base

15th February 1917

Dearest

I've been hanging on and on from day to day since I wrote you last, getting fresh orders to proceed, and each one has been cancelled. However we actually are going up this afternoon, and as I told you, to the 5th Camerons. So that is my new address. I was awfully bucked to get your budget with the photo of my dear wee son. I think it is stunning, the best I have. Thanks so much dear. It was good of you to write so much to me. I'm promising myself many reads of it up the line. Awfully sorry about Nancy. I'll write her when I get settled. We are all very pleased to get away from the base. It's rotten - too much work, and the cold has been at times unendurable. I'm glad to say it's a bit warmer now. The frost seems to have eased up a trifle. Well, my *belovedst* of all, I'll have to go and get lunch now, and then heigh-o for the line. Here's good fortune to us both anyhow.

All my love, my own girl. Yours to the end of the day and beyond,

Hugh

BEF

France

17th February 1917

Dearest Jess

Stuck again! We were banged down at a railhead yesterday, and found that the battalion was about six miles away. We were curiously enough expecting to be met, but that was our bally ignorance. We found about umpteen other people knocking around, but no Camerons. However we wired to the Adjutant for a limber and sat down to wait for it. Luck went against us after that, as when we had given up hope of its turning up and had gone to dinner, it arrived, and was gone before we got back. It was annoying, as we were stranded for the night. It was by no fault of ours, but we'll likely get chipped about it. Still, never mind! Nothing much matters when you get this length. We are still waiting for the rotten limber. My love to all, and especially to my wife and family.

Yours,

Hugh

France

20th February 1917

Dearest Jess

There has befallen a fearful accident of which we have just had word. It is officially announced that the mail-bags for the battalion took fire, and were burnt hopelessly, so I'm just afraid that I have lost a good few letters. I expect my surplus mail from the base has gone west in the conflagration. Very disgusting, isn't it, just when I was hoping to hear from you again.

We are still resting, and there is a yarn that we are going further back for more training for the push. The weather is still filthy wet and everything is over boot-tops in mud. I have had a platoon handed over to me, funnily enough No 13, same as my old one in the 7th. I hope I am to have the same luck this time as I had last. They are quite big fellows on the whole, but I shouldn't say they are the same standard or class of fellow as the old crowd. They are not so smart at drill as the old bunch, but I haven't seen them in the trenches yet and that is the main test after all.

I wrote Nancy Jarvie last night. Hope the wee lassie is better and about again. Well, doth the small son prosper, my dear? By the way hast thou had that done which we spoke of? If so, please let me know. I should be happier. There doesn't seem much more to say; the mess is full of smoke, and men playing bridge; and writing is an uneasy job with the racquet. My best love to the home circle, and heaps to you my darling lass, of whom I think always.

Yours,

Hugh

Hugh "somewhere in France"

France

26th February 1917

Dearest lassie

Good luck! Quite a lot of letters came up with the mail last night which had been lying at the base for me. It was as nice as ever to see your *hand-o-write* on one of them. I was at mess when the post came, and I nearly swallowed a teaspoon in my delight.

Glad you are fit and cheery, and the young *f'la* also. What times we shall have when this blessed business is over and done with, won't we, lass? I think every day of our little home that is to be. "As the river flows to the ocean" - do you remember the rest, petite? I am always in good form, thank goodness, so you don't need to worry about me at all. We were all sent to another village three days ago, and we are still in it. It is near the last one, so there was not a long march. Good thing too! About parcels, just send what you like, girlie. Our mess is quite good, but I haven't seen it in the trenches yet. So do what you think best, old lady, and I shall be only too delighted. We are still training hard for the big stunt, but as yet we know not the day nor the hour. Well, I'm for parade in ten minutes, so I'll have to shut down now, and not blether any more. All my love, sweetheart.

Yours ever,

Hugh

France

27th February 1917

Dearest Jess

I wrote you yesterday, but stupidly forgot to initial it, so I'm just afraid that it will have been torn up. So this is just a line in case to let you know that I still love you, and I'm still in the same place. Cheerio, girlie.

Your

Hugh

France

3rd March 1917

Dearest Jess

Another shift!!! This time can hear the rumble and roar of the guns round and behind us. Expect we are going into the line in a day or two, but in the meantime we are just behind it. If we are going in, it may be a day or two before you hear, but put it down to postal delays, please, and not to any more sinister cause.

Had a bad march yesterday, long road, heavy pack, and all the rest of the old game again. It was as pleasant as ever, but no good grousing, is there? So cheerio! My platoon's feet have been in a little trouble - lots of skinned heels, and fired soles. Things like that require constant attention. Comfy billet, and no complaints. I'll write soon again, but in the meantime three madmen are clamouring for me to complete a four at bridge.

Love to my own wee laddie, and to you, darling.

Yours ever,

Hugh

France

6th March 1917

Dearest Lass

Thanks for your last letter. Yes, my dear, by all means go and see Sutherland and his wife and give them both my warmest regards. Tell Lewis I only heard of his marriage quite recently, so he will require to forgive me for not writing him and wishing him happiness. I guess if he is as happy as you and I are, my darling, he will not grouse. I'm not very keen on his wife, but she may improve. The best point I ever saw in her was that she was about your size.

I'm awfully glad you are getting the wee boy christened. I wish I could have been there, but you will manage fine. Things go on as ever here, except that we are on men's rations now and not faring so well as when we were in rest. I can't tell you much, but we are well among the guns about 1,000 yards from the front line. It's wonderfully quiet here though and though we get a shell or so odd times, I'm glad to say I haven't had a casualty yet. Long may it continue.

Well dearie. Keep up your brave little heart and maybe it won't be so long before we see each other.

All my love,

Hugh

France

15th March 1917

Dearest Jess

Just a line to let you know that I am safely out of the trenches again with no casualties in my platoon. Others have not been so fortunate, and I am feeling very bucked. I'm terribly tired to-night, as the strain of an officer's job in the line is ever so much greater than that of a ranker, and I'm very short of sleep as well. So I'll tell you more next letter. But I thought you would be a bit anxious, so I write *toute de suite*. All my love, dearest,

Your husband

France

17th March 1917

Dearest Jess

I had a nice long letter from you yesterday giving me the very good news of the boy's christening. I am most awfully pleased about it, dear, and I'm sure you are also. Then I'm glad you enjoyed your visit to the Sutherlands so much. Lewis is an extremely good-hearted fellow, but very easily led. He will turn out very largely what his wife makes him. But then so will most of us, eh lass? It's fine to hear that Nancy Jarvie is better. Let's hope that she has no more turns like that.

Well, Jess, we are now having a nice rest after a particularly dirty spell in the line. The frost went suddenly one night, after which we had snow followed by rain, and the trenches fell in all over the place. This made one's spell of trench duty damned unpleasant. As we were being relieved one of my fellows got absolutely stuck in the mud in a Communication trench. He went in over the knees in glue, and it took four men and four rifles to lever him up. It got quite impassable higher up, and we ultimately climbed out and finished the journey over the top. Luckily it was a dull day, and Johnny's planes couldn't spot us. The Hun was pretty quiet while we were up. He seems to have the wind up badly in this sector and lives in mortal terror of the Jocks coming over for him. He did a bit of strafing with mortars and rather a beastly thing called a "Minnie". My Company had one man killed, but the other companies had several casualties. We are going up again on the 24th so here's to a continuance of our luck.

Isn't the war news good these days? We have just had a Comic Cuts wire to say that Bapaume has fallen. This is the sixth time in four days, but this time it is official. Good news too from Mesopotamia. Roll on peace! I guess it's getting nearer and nearer, and our little pictures will be coming up over the sky-line. Here's to it, sweetheart. Love to all.

Yours,

Hugh

France

20th March 1917

Dearest Jess

Thanks ever so much for the *bon* parcel from Coopers' which I got last night. Everything in it was top-hole and in the pink of condition. The photograph of Micky[17] was excellent, and say a thank you to the dear wee boy from his daddy for his letter.

Well, dearest, this note is to tell you not to be anxious if you don't hear for a week or so. We are going up to-morrow, but don't know whether it's an ordinary tour of duty or a fight. So this is just an "in case" note. I'll keep you as well posted as I can. I'm awfully busy making arrangements, so I'll stop. You have all my love and thoughts, lass.

Ever your boy

France
23rd March 1917

Dearest Jess

We are at the war again, but still nothing much doing. Artillery going it a trifle perhaps. The weather is rather chilly, but it's the war I expect. Well, hope it will soon be all over, girlie, so that I can get back to you. It can't come soon enough, can it? Well, cheerio, dearie.

Yours,

Hugh

France
24th March 1917

Dearest Lass

Just a line again to let you know that I am all right and in the pink. There has been nothing doing in the way of going over the top, and we are going back into town to-night. It has been moderately quiet here, though we caught the tail of one or two strafes. Nothing to make a song and dance about however. I'll be getting a letter from you I should think by to-night's mail. There's one about due. Hurrah! Well, my dearest love to you both.

Your husband always,

Hugh

France
28th March 1917

Dearest Jess

Back again! We spent the last four days in a town just behind the line, and now after a considerable period of "wind-up" we are resting. It was very warm in the last place, as Fritz took revenge for a number of raids by shelling the town vigorously. However we are now well out of the shell zone for the time being. We were amiably quarrelling over a game of bridge two afternoons ago when one plumped through the billet. Somehow the game lost its interest after that. Still not every one comes as close as that, and in any case *c'est la guerre*. We had violent working-parties every night up there also. It is always the same near the line. One is always on some bally thing or other, if one is not actually in the line. However we never complain overmuch lest a worse thing befall. Good principle ain't it? Well, dear, it is a beastly day of lashing rain and a cold wind! Also we have not long marched in, so I'll buzz off, I think. We haven't had a mail for two days now - God knows why. We are living in hopes for to-night though. All my love, dearest.

Yours always,

Hugh

France

2nd April 1917

Dearest Jess

Thanks very much for your last long letter. I'm so glad everything is going well with you and the boy. We are having a very quiet time at present back in rest and there is really nothing to indicate that there is a war on. I suppose, though we shall be well in the middle of it shortly. We expected it last time we were up, but it didn't come off. The weather latterly has been something chronic - cold and driving sleet and rain with a wind blowing straight from the pole. Have sent back a lot of togs also in the pious hope that the weather would improve. I expect it will come all right in a week or so. Well, roll on peace, old girl. All my love.

Yours ever,

Hugh

Hugh, middle row second from right, and friends. Date unknown.

Chapter 2

"One cannot get away from the fact that France is an entirely unhealthy residential area at the moment."

The brigade's first attack on Arras began on 9 April. The 9th Scottish Division "side-stepped" the River Scarpe and prepared for battle. The Cameron Highlanders were to take part in the final wave of the attack. The Division met with considerable success while the 5th Battalion lost only eighty-five rank and file members and one officer was wounded. Although the battalion returned to billets in Y Huts on the 15th, it appears that Hugh's platoon was stranded in the trenches for a further few days. On the 21st the battalion travelled by train to very comfortable billets at Terna, returning to Y Huts on the 25th before rejoining the battle.

France
5th April 1917

Dearest Jess

Just a wee note to let you know that we are going up the line again to-morrow. So the old remark applies - if you don't hear for a bit don't worry. I'm not going to write much as I'm stuck in bed to-day with a chill, and we want it to go by to-morrow. I think we are on the job this time, but a day or two will tell. All love to you and sonnie boy.

Ever yours,

Hugh

France
18th April 1917

Dearest Jess

I have time to write you only a short note, as I am up to the neck in making up platoon deficiencies. In addition to which if I started in to tell you of the happenings of last week, my friend the Censor would step in. We had a very rough week of it. On Monday morning (ten days ago) we went over the top after the most intense and hellish bombardment you ever conceived. Had very few casualties indeed, and drove Fritz back about five miles. Pretty good work and we were all pleased about it. Then when we expected to be relieved it didn't come off and we were knocking about up there for eight days. The last three we spent in the furthest advanced trenches - or alleged trenches with aeroplanes coming hooting over all the time to see how the line ran. We were shelled to hell day and night - a most beastly time. However we are all out now, and resting. How long we shall be out I do not know, but here's to us anyhow. No luck for a *blighty* one so far. Hope you are all well. All my love, dearest.

Hugh

France

22nd April 1917

Dearest Jess

Thanks ever so much for your Ardeonaig letter which rolled up last night. You wrote some time ago of a parcel you had ordered from MacEwen's, but as it has not come along, possibly it has gone astray in the confusion of the push. I do hope not, and perhaps it may turn up yet. I've just discovered some ink and as it's a great pleasure to use it again, I'll break into it. I'm awfully glad you are all having such a happy time up there and I hope the filthy weather will do a stagger for you. It will be another case of not knowing the boy when I see him again. I looked out very earnestly for a *blighty* one in that push of ours, but nothing happened and I'm still with the company. I'm told that my Invergordon friend, Hay, got his cushy one with the 6th and is now doubtless in England. Sorry you haven't had news of Howard yet, but you are sure to presently. It's hard enough to keep up decent communications here, so one can see what a job it must be in Egypt. The eight days we were in the show I managed to get one p.c. off to you, and there wasn't one other chance at any time till we came out. You say Arnold is not certain of his position. Tell him from me to make sure that it is somewhere in the British Isles, and he needn't worry about anything else. One cannot get away from the fact that France is an entirely unhealthy residential area at the moment, and he has already done his whack and secured his *blighty* one. A fellow can get one with luck; twice, the Lord has looked on him; but thrice is an apocalyptic but not the less genuine miracle.

How are Winnie's tootsies getting along? All right, I hope. Give her my best and a lusty Cheerio! By the way I've never explained (1) the ink, (2) the long letter, (3) the general cheerfulness with which I am imbued. Explanation follows *toute de suite*. We entrained yesterday, and came away down the line for a rest. We are a good thirty kilos behind the line and can only hear the guns when there is a big side strafe on. The engine-driver of our train, who I am convinced was a holy angel carefully and adequately disguised, drew up at a placid little siding, and dumped this noble battalion. From there we walked a few miles through golden gates straight into paradise. In earthy parlance it is a little village pleasantly mixed up with the pleasantest of roads and fields. It is clean like fairyland, though I suspect the scavengers were His Majesty's troops. All the fields are green, and the hedges are blossoming. The sun is shining like hell, and the world looks very beautiful and full of joy to me. I have a charming billet with a comfy bed and table and fire when the cool evening rolls up. Also madame, my landlady, is portly and apple-cheeked, with the whitest and most regular teeth. The men are very well housed too, and everything in the garden is lovely. Matter of fact, this is the first sign of spring we have had, after coming thro' a weary hell of fighting on desolate landscapes, and suffering all the evil turns weather could inflict. So we are all more than a little mad with the *joie de vivre*. We shall get over it all right, but *pour le moment* we rejoice openly.

You never mention jolly old finance, but I guess you will if you run short or anything: 'cos I can easily send you a cheque at any time, old lady. All my love, dearest,

Hugh

France
26th April 1917

Dearest Jess

Thanks so much for your letter from Tayside which I got last night. I'm awfully sorry about your cold, old lady, but I hope by the time you get this it will be long past. The weather will have bucked up, and everything will be lovely in the garden except the rhubarb. Well, dear, we are away from that bonnie village I told you of, and back up the line. It is not pleasant to go up after coming out. Still, mustn't grumble. I've had a lot of friends killed since the 9th and I know how lucky I am so far. The battalion is going up - all the way - to-morrow, but as I'm acting second-in-command of the Company I may be left with the transport to replace casualties. This is a usual thing, but we are short of subs and I may be in it again.

I'm in haste now dear one. All my love. Ever yours,

Hugh

France
29th April 1917

Dearest Jess

Just the *weeniest* note to let you know that I am still in the pink. I got left out of this show as second-in-command, and I hope I shall not have to go up, as if I have to, Cameron will have become a casualty. I am also going to a Lewis Gun Course in a few days which will last about seven days. The weather is excellent now - warm and sunny, but the fighting is very severe and heavy. We are all optimists in these days, and it's very likely that the whole affair will be over this summer. God grant it. Well, I'm very busy looking after the fellows up the line, and seeing that they are properly fed, and so forth. All my love, dear.

Yours,

Hugh

Chapter 3

"I had a splendid time on the Lewis Gun Course but all the time I was worried about the Company and my platoon especially, and I hadn't much heart to write home."

On 1 May the battalion took up positions north of Faupoux. The battalion's second attack at Arras should have met with at least as much success as their first, but unfortunately from the very beginning things went wrong with officers being wounded as they moved up the line. The enemy's position was not clear and to make matters worse, a strategic enemy position, the Chemical Works at Roeux, had not been put out of action as planned. As a result German machine-guns mowed down advancing troops. Half an hour from the beginning of the attack the battalion had already lost all but two officers and about ninety men. Hugh's Company Captain, Archie Cameron, the brother of The Lochiel who had raised the Cameron regiments in August 1914, was killed. The final toll of casualties on 10 May was 18 officers and 300 men. The battalion retired to Y Huts on 11 May, marching to Penin the next day and from there to billets at Chelers. The men were kept busy with training and with fitness and morale boosting competitions at Chelers until the 30th when they travelled in buses to Arras and from there returned once more to the trenches.

The Lewis Gun for which Hugh was being trained was a light machine gun developed in the United States which had become by this time the most widely used machine gun among the British and Empire battalions. In 1915 only four Lewis guns would have been available for each battalion but by 1917 a battalion would have had thirty-six guns as well as specialist Lewis-gunners. The gun was fed from a circular drum which held either 47 or 97 rounds and could fire 500 rounds a minute.

Lewis machine gun

France
13th May 1917

Dearest Jess

You have been favoured recently by your loving husband with letters of the scrappiest order, while you have been acting the true wee wife by keeping me splendidly posted. Thanks so much, darling, for your lovely letters. I guess you know how much they mean to me - they are just fragrant with your dear self, and sometimes in these bonnie nights I can hear you speaking, and see the light in your dear eyes. Well, girlie, the reason I have not written so regularly is that I have been anxious and unhappy to a degree. I had a splendid time on that Lewis Gun Course but all the time I was worried about the Company and my platoon especially, and I hadn't much heart to write home. I have now to-night joined the battalion, and find things just about what I expected. They have had a rough time, and I feel very sorry that I was not with them. We have 3 officers killed, 15 wounded and 2 missing. Capt. Cameron, my Company officer is missing, and all the subs who went up are wounded. In fact the man who took my platoon over has not been traced to any hospital, and fears are entertained for his safety. My platoon is about 10 strong. Isn't it damnable? They got up against a nest of machine-guns, and were knocked over like flies. A sub is now in command of my Company, and I am 2nd in command. But I do not think it will be for long, as we expect some Captains and 2 pip merchants in a draft, in which case, of course I return to my platoon.

Well, lassie, I was glad indeed to hear of Arnold's fixity of tenure, and he should stick to it. The fewer intimate friends I have out here just now the better I am pleased. It's grand also to hear of Howard's good time - which he is due and overdue. About your parcel, girlie, I was away at the time it rolled up, and it was sent to the officers in the advanced line. I am sure you will not be vexed at this, as you can guess their need. Also darling, I don't want you to send out much as I can see that things at home are in a bad way, and prices are prohibitive. So long as you send me your love, wee love-lass, that is all I require. This is in spots a sloppy letter for an old married man, but I must tell you sometimes how I love you.

Ever yours,

Hugh

France
20th May 1917

Darling Jess

I have your letter telling me about Howard's coming. How absolutely topping for you all! I'm so glad the weather is decent, and so forth. See and give him a damn good time, for I guess he'll be needing it after that long spell in Egypt. I expect he will hardly know Micky, will he? Give him my best. I only wish I was along with you. Still, mustn't grumble!

We are still in rest in this jolly little stinking village, but I don't know for how long. I think they'll give us as long as possible, as nerves need rest, but old Fritz over the way has been pretty free with his counter-bumps lately, and we may be for the dirty work *bientôt*. I'm doing Lewis Gun Officer at the moment, but I expect to go back to the Company, when we go up the line. The job keeps me pretty busy as we lost over 60% of our trained gunners that last spell, and it's the devil training new hands in a short time. Still we're getting on with it.

Love to all. Yours ever,

Hugh

> On Active Service
> WITH THE BRITISH EXPEDITIONARY FORCE
> YMCA
> France
> 28th May 1917

Dearest Jess

One line only! I am at GHQ Lewis Gun School at Le Touquet for 5 days and as well as being very busy the heat is hopeless. I'm one grease spot. I'll write when I rejoin regiment and receive my letters which won't be for five or six days. All my love dearie,

Your sun-smitten Mann

> France
> 1st June 1917

Dearest

Back to the battalion after a most topping time, and I have neglected the bit wife shamefully. I can't even make up for it at the moment, as I'm just going up to join the Company in the line. But I'm hoping it will be sufficiently peaceful to let me get a decent letter written to you.

I had a splendid five days at Le Touquet, golfing, bathing and so forth, but of that more anon. I'm so glad you are all having such good times with Howard.

Cheerio, dearie *pour le moment.*

Yours always,

Hugh

Chapter 4

"Every company officer is now dead, and fifteen subs casualties. What a hope!"

Hugh rejoins his battalion on 1 June while it is in reserve trenches. His Company moves to Crump Trench, west of Roeux where the enemy is subjected to heavy shelling. On the 5th two of Hugh's men were killed and a number injured in a foray into 'no man's land' which led to the successful capturing of 220 Germans. The battalion suffered heavy shelling for the next few days and menacing air activity forced the use of the Lewis gun teams for anti-aircraft defence. While in the front-line at this point, Sir Harry Lauder paid the battalion a visit during which, by special request, he sang for the men until forced to an abrupt halt by a sudden outburst of German shelling. The men then moved to reserve positions at the Railway Embankment near Fampoux close to the front line. When they were relieved by another battalion on the 12th, they marched to Arras and proceeded from there in motor wagons to Orlencourt and Moncy Breton in the neighbourhood of Ruellecourt, then on to Beaufort and Warlus. In all they spent a whole month in billets. It was during this period that Hugh officially became commander of his Company.

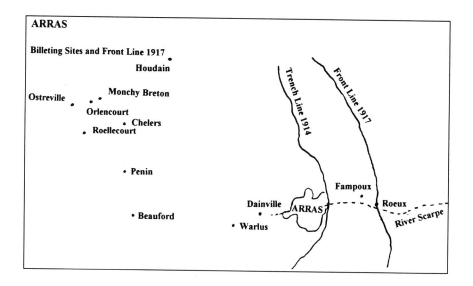

France

7th June 1917

Dearest Jess

We have been in a few days now, and having a pretty thin time. There has been a stunt on our immediate right, and things have been damnably peevish since. I had a rough night last night with a working-party: got caught in a Hun barrage and lost two killed and five wounded. We were pretty lucky, and got off lightly. However one mustn't talk shop all the time. We expect to come out in a few days, at which there will be general rejoicing.

The weather has been extremely hot and clammy. I'm glad you had such a *bon* time with old Howard. And the news that Arnold and May are going to be married. I will write you about that when I get out of the line. I'll send you a wee cheque and you will get what they desire as a wedding-gift from us.

I'm short of sleep a lot, and going to get down to it now. All my love, darling.

Yours,

Hugh

France

13th June 1917

Darling Jess

Please excuse my delay in answering your last letter, and enclosing cheque. Trouble was I was in a very tight place for the last four days, in a situation which wanted most careful watching. We expected the old bosche over any time, and altogether had a hell of a rotten trip. However we are out now, and just four hours into our peaceful rest village. So you will absolve me from neglecting your letter, won't you dear?

I enclose cheque for £4 which will cover your needs, and also a present for Arnold and May when the time comes. See and get something nice for these nice people, won't you?

I have a fine billet here in a bonnie wee garden, and the pleasure of crawling into sheets is something to look forward to to-night. Jove, we had a rough spell that last time - shelled like stink every day and night. Thank the Lord we are out for a *whilie*.

All my love, dear. Post's just going, and I don't want to miss him. Yours,

Hugh

France

17th June 1917

Dearest Jess

Thanks for your letter which I got to-day. Did I tell you how nice the two wee photos were? They were delicious, old darling and took me right home to you. It is hard to realize that I haven't seen either of you for nearly five months.

I was bucked to get the invitation to the wedding reinforced by Nina and Winnie. I told the Brigadier that there would be Hell to pay if I didn't get leave for it, but he said my story was sad but old - 2 years and 10 months old. So I fear it cannot *was*. Doesn't the war sometimes strike you as damn silly, and a *helofa* waste of time? Another of our officers has just died of wounds from the 3rd of May stunt. I was mortal lucky to be out of that show. Every Company Officer is now dead, and 15 subs casualties. What a hope!

The men are getting well rested from that last beastly spell in the line. I never saw them so jumpy and on edge before. It was the constant shelling with big stuff, and seeing people going up in the air. They are much better now though. The Company Officer is in hospital for four or five days, and I have the Coy at the moment. It's good fun but wearing.

All my love, sweetheart. Yours,

Hugh

France

28th June 1917

Dearest Jess

Still sticking it well - in rest billets. It is a hard life, but very enjoyable - heaps of training, and so forth, and then all sorts of sports. We have also been much disturbed and perturbed by the pervading presence of Brigadiers and other unpleasant critical people. D Coy won the Regimental sports by a long chalk, and now we have Brigade ones coming off next Tuesday. We start training about 6.30, and this involves getting up at the back of five. *No bon, ch?*

Well, I'm glad the wedding went off so well, and I wish to goodness I had been there to enjoy it with you. I consumed the wedding cake with much gusto and jolly good it was too.

I don't seem to have much to say to you, old girl - reason being I fancy that the hour is 7 a.m., and we are standing by till the rain goes off to do a battalion stunt. Still I can always say the old thing.

Fondest love. Ever yours,

Hugh

See and get something for Arnold too.

France

8th July 1917

Dearie

Thanks ever so for your long newsy letter. Glad you are enjoying Tayside again. Gee, I wish I were walking by your side up the *burnie*.

We have done another shift nearer the line, but still no sign of active service. I am still OC Coy, as Noble is still in hospital. He is wangling it fine, and I wish to God he would come back, as I haven't the faintest chance of leave till he returns. I'm over six months in France now, and three months overdue for leave. A damned shame I call it.

Depressed to-night dearie, so won't write more in case I depress you too.

All love,

Hugh

France

9th July 1917

Darlingest wee wifie,

I got your soul-scorching letter to-day. You must have missed a letter, for I'm DAMNED sure I never let thirteen days pass without writing you. I wrote yesterday, and I write again to-day, this time to wish you many happy and ever happier returns of your dear birthday. May you and I spend many of them together. What a nice letter from Davie McQueen. We must all go and see him some day. If my letters have been short and sweet lately, it's partly because I'm busy, and more because I'm just a bit fed up. I've been through some roughish passages, and several times resigned myself to a crown and a harp at the *toute de suite,* and I suppose it's got just a tiny bit on my nerves. However I'll be all right again once I get my leave - whenever the devil that will be.

Well, dearie, *beaucoup pour ce temps.* Love to boy and you. Yours,

Hugh

From Jessie's album circa July 1917. Duncan Cameron Mann with his Aunt, Alison Hetherington, and her young son Scott

France

14th July 1917

Dearest Jess

My days are so extraordinarily full just now that I have to put spurs in my side often to remind me that I am due you a letter. We are still resting - by Jove it has been some rest too - over a month since we were at the war, and still no word of anything doing. We had fine Brigade Sports two days ago, and the good old Camerons had a pukka field-day, picking up nearly everything that mattered. Since then it has been the old story - early parades and heaps to do. I'm still in charge of the Company, and there is no word of Noble coming back yet. It's no bother now though, as so much of the work is routine. I hope you've been having decent weather. We have had a lot of rain, and occasional thunder-storms.

Well, cheerio, old lady. All love to the family and you. Yours,

Hugh

France

18th July 1917

My dearest Jess

Thanks so much for the lovely photos of the boy. They are extraordinarily good. I think his hair must be getting a lot darker. It seems so in the photo anyhow. By Jove, he does look healthy and sturdy, and his legs are like the pillar of Heracles. It's fine to get such good likenesses of the wee sonnie.

I'm glad you are enjoying such a nice-time, and I hope you will be strong and fit in the *bon* hill air. At this end of our live wire things are going peacefully so far. All the men are bucked at getting such a splendid long rest, for there have been several dirty shows that we might have been in. From all we hear we are going in somewhere about the 25th, but like everything else here, it is uncertain. Still everyone will go in now with their tails up ready to give old Fritz a thin time. I'm still commanding the Coy, but several people are expected back who will relieve me. I've had the Coy a month now, and I was supposed at first to have it four or five days. I've enjoyed the experience immensely, and if we get a heavy battering with a hell of a lot of casualties, and if I get through, I might get the job permanently. Good few "ifs" about it though.

What I've liked as much as anything has been having a horse of my own. I must have ridden miles in the last month. It's really great sport, and fine exercise.

Well, dearie, I've to go, and spectate at a platoon football match now. All my love.

Yours,

Hugh

France

22nd July 1917

Dearest Jess

Thanks ever so much for your long letter with the nice wee photo of boy. It is like the others awfully good. I'm glad you are having such a nice time, good weather and so forth. It's just the same here now - every day sun shining most violently. It's really far too hot for parades. We are still here but move on Wednesday to pastures new. Everybody is pleased that we are for a change of front. That place up the line where we have been practically six months has scunnered us all. You will be getting a photo. Hope you like it. Still no word of leave, alas!

   There was a battalion officer's dinner last night and hence the disjointed nature of my remarks. Cheerio old dear.

Yours,

Hugh

B. E. F.

'France

17. 2. 17.

Dearest Jess,

Stuck again! We were banged down at a railhead yesterday, + found that the battalion was about 6 miles away. We were curiously enough expecting to be met, but that was our bally ignorance. We found about umpteen other people knocking around, but no Camerons. However we wired to the Adjutant for a limber, + sat down to wait for it. Luck went against us after that, as when we had given up hope of its turning up + had gone to dinner, it arrived, + was gone before we got back. It was annoying, as we were stranded for the night. It was by no fault of ours, but well likely get chipped about it. Still, never mind! Nothing much matters when you get this length. We are still waiting for the rotten limber. My love to all, + specially to my wife + family.

Yours. Hugh. —

Chapter 5

"It's one thing to have a platoon in the line, and another to be responsible for a company sector on the Western Front."

On 25 July the battalion returned to the trenches where the men experienced a relatively quiet spell until they were moved by train to Ruyaulcourt on 2 August from where they returned to the trenches at Havrincourt on the 7th. Between then and the 16th the battalion was fairly active on the front while facing considerable activity from enemy artillery.

Hugh's long-overdue leave must have materialised at last some time late in August. He had spent over seven months at the Front. The usual leave entitlement was one week which for Scottish soldiers with long distances to travel was far too short. Hugh had initially been due to set off again for the Front on Sunday 1 September but a request for an extension appears to have been granted.

France

31st July 1917

Dearest Jess

Thanks ever so much for your nice letters. I do hope you are by this time at Pirnmill, the good old mill, and having a top-hole time of it. Well, dearie, we have now been down *les tranchées* four days, and the game is quite good. The wily Hun is very peaceful down in these parts, and on the whole desires only to be left alone. I am still OC D Coy, and with a large slice of luck may keep it. But it is still on the knees of the gods. In the meantime I'm enjoying it fine, though sometimes one gets a bit anxious. It's one thing to have a platoon in the line, and another to be responsible for a company sector of the Western Front. Well, I'm not idle, so excuse all but my love to you and the sonnie boy.

Yours,

Hugh

3rd August 1917

Darling Girlie

A wee line to let you know that we are now out for eight days' rest. The billets are no good, as the old Hun blew up everything here as he retired. But the line is very cushy. Much work to be done on it, but very little risk of premature decease which makes a welcome change from that horrible spot Roeux.

Glad you will be having a good time at Pirnmill. By the way there is no word of my leave yet, and it's looking none too good.

All my love dearie, to you and the boy. Yours,

Hugh

France

6th August 1917

Dearest Lassie

Here we are, and to-morrow night we again go into the line, and there is still no prospect of leave. Isn't it disgusting? Our chaplain is away to-night, and it is exactly four months since his previous leave!!! Still, mustn't grouse, I suppose.

We have had five quiet days in reserve, nothing doing but working-parties at night. I've had one or two nice rides across country, and manage to keep fairly fit that way. The part we go into isn't quite so nice as the last place. It is the front line or rather a funny part to hold, but I'm hoping it will be nice and quiet. There is one nice development. I have got the Company for good now - at least so those slippery people at Headquarters say. They have not put me through orders however, and so I won't get back pay for it till they do. Still it's not so bad, girlie, is it?

I'm very short of officers, having only two for the line this time. One is on a course and two are sick. It's the devil being so short, as it means that those who are there have a lot of work, long spells of duty and so forth.

And how are you getting on at Pirnmill? By Jove, I can see you, and the nipper hurling yourselves about on the sand. God, don't I wish I was there with you both. Still we can't have everything, can we? I was reading old Lloyd George's speech about the end of the war, and was beginning to feel mighty bucked and hopeful, till a chit came in from the Division offering a prize for the best design for a Divisional X'mas card! That's rather a drop, isn't it?

All my love and thought to both you dears. Yours,

Hugh

10th August 1917

Dearest Wifie

I had your jolly letter from Pirnmill and gee! Couldn't I just see the water splashing round you two kippers? What times you must be having, my own wee lassie. I am afraid sometimes I grudge to this wretched war the time I might be spending with you two dears. Still we *canna* help it, can we? I am back to the cave-dwelling mode of life three days now. It is not very thrilling, but at times the responsibility keeps one anxious. One has about five thousand things per day to remember and to do when a Coy is in the line. Still it's worth it I think, and I'd rather have a Coy than a platoon any time.

The weather has been rather better lately, but very changeable. One goes out to go round the line in beautiful sunshine, and clear skies, and before you get half round, a heavy rain is drowning you. Still it's all in the life.

I have no more word about leave but the Adjutant was up this afternoon and asked how long I had been out. He said he was going to send some officers on leave soon. So that looks a wee bit more healthy.

Well, cheerio, old lady, and let's hear from you soon. Ever yours,

Hugh

(Hugh's hopes of leave must have been realised as there are no further letters from France until September.)

2 London St

Edinburgh

Wednesday night

Dearie

It's getting on, and I've collected a headache, let alone a wee heart ache, but I must send you just a line. It's for Sunday the first after all, and I've been making the wires hot with indignant requests for an extension. I haven't the least idea whether I'll get it or not, but I'm hoping for the best. I had not too bad a journey down, quite a decent train.

I want to tell you of the memories of love and infinite tenderness of the week we had together. My darling, I'll never forget it, and I think of it as just a foretaste of what is to come. Keep up your brave heart, my lass. It'll all come right yet.

Love to Mama, and to my own dear wee sonnie boy. Heart's love to you, my precious one. Yours always,

Hugh

2 London St

Edinburgh

13th September 1917

My darling Jess

Voici the little note you asked for. Well, I got through A1 on Tuesday, and have since paid two more visits to the darned old dentist. He has left the grinders in good order, and their sound should now be low. I've also paid expensive calls on outfitters, and innumerable relatives, as I'm now at the morning of my last day. Leave is a good thing, but like most good things it has a fleeting way with it. As I said to you often, the only thing worth having is a damn good *blighty* one. Tim is in this morning, and I've told him your message and he is hoping to get through for a day or two after the harvest. I also told mother your message. They both send love. And you know what I send, don't you, old thing? My love to the boy from his long-suffering daddy. And all to you.

Hugh

P.S. My old woman's a DAM FOOL!

The last photograph taken of Hugh with his young
son, Duncan Cameron (Micky)

PART VI

Before and After Passchendaele: September 1917 - November 1917

Passchendaele from *Yuletide Greetings from the Cameron Highlanders* sent to Jessie, Christmas 1918

Field Marshall Sir Douglas Haig's next target was the Ypres Salient, which, since the First Battle of Ypres in 1914, had seen the deaths of thousands of British soldiers. The ill-informed War Cabinet, although reluctant at first, finally supported Haig's venture which from the start was doomed to failure. The Salient had become a quagmire from the wettest August since 1878 and although September was not excessively wet, it rained almost daily the following month until 13 October. By the end of July a million German soldiers, well aware of Haig's plans for an attack, were ready to confront a million of their British counterparts. The offensive which began on 31 July continued relentlessly until 10 November. On 12 October, the day of the main offensive known as the First Battle of Passchendaele, conditions on the approach to, and on Passchendaele Ridge itself, were dire. The rain fell heavily while shells churned up the quagmire so that men struggled to advance as they sank waist-deep in mud. Many soldiers drowned in the mud, some of the injured were left to die and the treatment of others was delayed. Following a final attack on 7 November, the British line was even more awkwardly placed than before and by then British casualties numbered over 300,000 while German casualties came to 200,000.

A muddy First World War trench near Ypres June 1998

Chapter 1

"As my Company is leading the whole proceedings, I am hoping this time to secure a nice reasonable blighty to put me over the winter."

Hugh returned from leave to find his battalion had moved to a new area in Belgium. He joined his men at their billeting huts at the Toronto Camp near Brandhoek. The battalion's first involvement in the Battle of Passchendaele was on 20 September. The men disembarked at a siding called Goldfish Chateau outside Ypres, bivouacked in pouring rain and then passed through the Menin Gate. Beyond the Gate they left the road and set off across country. The going was slow and difficult because of the darkness, shell-holes, barbed wire and mud. For the next three days the men were in the thick of fierce shelling, gas and air attack. Even as they retreated along the road back to Ypres, German shells were dropping at the rate of three or four a minute. Between shells, gas sickness, bolting mules, and numerous obstacles such as dead horses on the road, they were lucky to survive. Despite their grim circumstances the battalion's part in the attack was considered a great success and their loss relatively small with a total of 112 casualties. A tooth abscess had however stopped Hugh from leading his Company on this occasion.

The battalion retired to billets at Wormhoudt, west of Ypres, then moved briefly to the Front again before billeting at Eringhem in houses and farm buildings to rest and prepare for the next engagement at Passchendaele, this time at the northern end of the ridge. The attack had been fixed for 5.35 on 12 October but victory at Passchendaele was becoming increasingly unlikely as the mud deepened and the rain continued on a battlefield covered with fortified farms and pill-boxes which meant the men would be easy targets for German machine gun fire. On the 11th the 5th battalion left the security of their billets, took a train to Brielen, and marched the rest of the way to their positions. Difficult and tedious progress in the pouring rain on slippery duckboards was made worse when one of the guides lost his way and consequently subjected the men to an extra four hours of exhausting wandering in mud and dark. The chaos and mismanagement of Loos in 1915 were repeated and failure was inevitable when most of the officers became casualties on the first day. The field dressing stations were unable to cope with the injured and on the night of the 12th/13th thirty injured soldiers had to be left outside the dressing station at Burns House all night and about twenty others were left in shell holes. The 5th Battalion's casualties came to over 200 dead, wounded or missing in one day.

The next day, the 13th, the battalion withdrew to Hubner Farm away from the unspeakable conditions of mud, shells and pouring rain. A week later the survivors marched in stages to billets at Zuydcoote on the coast.

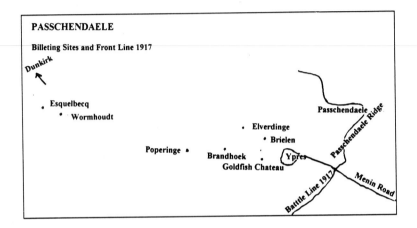

France

Sunday

Dearest Jess

Here I am back in this ruddy country once more. I had a very decent journey to London and alas! the train was in superb time and I had no chance of swanking a buckshee day at all. I was OC of a troop train down to Folkestone and Adjutant of the boat in which we crossed. So I was on duty all the time. Damn bad luck but I shall know what to avoid next time. Then I had practically no time to do anything in Boulogne as my train left at 12.50 a.m., a truly horrible hour. Early next morning I was dumped down at railhead and soon found the Battalion. As I suspected, we have moved to a new area. We are still out of the line but go up in a day or two for some fun with brother Bosche. So we are really back to the war with a vengeance.

Well dearie, I suppose in a week or two, especially if it is strenuous, my memories of my leave will be dimmer, but just now they are fresh. Thank you so much darling for the good time you gave me. It was just like a bit of heaven all the time.

My love to everyone, especially Chicko and yourself. Ever yours,

Hugh

France

18th

Dearest Jess

I have so much to do in arranging things for our little effort that I hardly know where to turn first. Still I must get this tiny note away before things begin to happen. The weather is dull, but mercifully fair so far. Now you are not to worry if you have no letter for a week or two. I'll send p.cs as soon as possible. My best love to all - especially Micky boy, and your dear self.

Ever your husband,

Hugh

France

21st

Dearest Jess

Worst luck of the war. I developed a hell of an abscess at the root of my tooth, and my face and mouth were in such a state that the Doctor wouldn't let me go up. I was terribly distressed about it, but in truth I wasn't fit to command men. I was distracted with the thing. I had the tooth pulled by an Australian doctor, and some lancing done, and it is a little better to-day. I hope to get up the line in a day or two. Meantime I am grieved beyond words.

All my love to both you dears. Yours,

Hugh

France

1st October 1917

Dearest

1st of October! Aren't the days and months passing. Thanks for your last letter which told me of your well-being. Things have been quieter with us these last few days. We were up the line again in support, but it was not serious as we were not required. Now we are back for a few days in a nice peaceful clean little village, wherein I have a most excellent billet, and altogether I am quite pleased with life. To-morrow I go away for three days to some Corps lectures on the next strafe, so I shan't be writing you for a day or so.

All my love to boy and you. Yours,

Hugh

France

7th October 1917

My darling Jess

Thanks ever so much for your last two letters. The photo I like awfully. I did not think that sonnie was laughing like that at the time, but there's no doubt about it. Well, dear, I had three good interesting days at the Corps School and learnt a lot about how the war is going. Then to-morrow we go up nearer the line and in a few days we are going into action. As my Company is leading the whole proceedings, I am hoping this time to secure a nice reasonable *blighty* to put me over the winter. I'm most concerned about the weather which has gone broke these last four days. To-day it's a howling gale with lashing unceasing rain. This kind of thing makes moving about in the bogs and shell-holes of a Flanders battle-field vastly unpleasant.

Well, I see I was gazetted Captain dated June 7th, so I'll be getting some nice back pay one of these days. Meantime a wee cheque to cheer you up at the beginning of winter, with all my love and thoughts.

Well, cheerio, girlie. Kiss the boy for his daddy. Yours,

Hugh

The railway station at Esquelbecq 1998 from which Hugh set off for his final battle at Passchendaele

Ardeonaig c.1896 and c.1906

Chapter 2

"All my love, precious, to you and my darling boy."

Hugh was not to make it to Zuydcoote however. At some point on the 12th he was seriously injured and two days later was taken to the Hôpital Général Anglais No 3 at Les Terrasses in Le Tréport on the Normandy Coast. Jessie was not informed for another five days that Hugh had been wounded. He fought his painful injuries for a month but he died in hospital on 12 November 1917.

The Hospital at Le Tréport on the Normandy coast to which Hugh was taken following the Battle of Passchendaele. The hospital was surrounded by tents to accommodate injured soldiers when the hospital was full.

The cause of his death is not certain but it appears to have been caused by either gangrene or gas gangrene. Gas gangrene had nothing to do with gas warfare but developed when bacteria from richly manured farmland entered a wound. The wound would putrefy and inflate like a balloon full of gas. Gas gangrene killed even those with relatively minor wounds in far greater numbers than actual gas during the First World War as antibiotics had not yet been invented and the newly developed antiseptics were not very effective. The best form of treatment was to remove damaged tissue as soon as possible. For Hugh, delay in receiving adequate treatment and being hospitalised might have proved fatal or perhaps his wound could have been such that all damaged tissue could not in any case have been removed.

In the normal course of events an injured soldier would first of all be taken to the nearest first aid post and from there to the advanced dressing station for an anti-tetanus jab. There would then follow a bone-shaking ride to the nearest hospital by motor ambulance or cart. British soldiers were often taken slowly and circuitously by rail to hospitals such as Hôpital Général Anglais No 3 on the chalk cliffs of Le Tréport.

Hugh had received his "blighty". The letter dated 19 October is Hugh's last known letter. Although clearly seriously injured, he is not at this point expecting to die. Furthermore, his handwriting is as clear and legible as ever.

Telegram 17th October 1917
War Office London
OHMS

To: Mrs Mann, Bertrohill, Shettleston, Glasgow.

Regret to inform you that Capt H.W. Mann Cameron Hghrs admitted three general Hospital Letreport Oct thirteenth with gunshot wound left thigh severe further reports will be sent on receipt

Sec. War Office

France
19th October 1917

Dearest Jess

As my last note, if I recollect alright, was rather a gloomy effort, I write so soon again to let you know that I am getting on famously. My wounds are not so sore, though the whole leg is useless and last night for the first time I slept a bit without any sleeping-draught and had almost no temperature. This morning the world looks very beautiful, and full of joy to me. One gets accustomed after a few days to lying all the time in a constrained position. Indeed when I come home you'll probably find that I won't be able to sleep without a huge air-pillow under my left flank, and the right, about a foot lower. I'm still tied up by getting no news from anywhere. There must be a lot of letters addressed to me knocking about France somewhere, but so far none has found me out. I've still no prospect of getting across or no word at any rate. It doesn't matter a bit though 'cos I'm perfectly happy here and I know I'll get sometime which is the main thing. If I get to London, I'm going to write Arnold and he might do the good Samaritan and look me up. I've forgotten his address but - North? Chelmsford, Essex, will find him, won't it?

All my love, precious, to you and my darling boy. Yours, Hugh

63. LES TERRASSES — Hôpital Général Anglais N° 3
British Général Hospital N° 3

Chapter 3

"However we're back to it again and we'll have to live in our letters until the next time, haven't we?" (Jessie)

Unaware of the tragedy of Passchendaele, Jessie continued her regular missives to Hugh. She wrote eight letters to Hugh between 12 September when his leave ended, and 18 October when she must have received a letter from Hugh which is missing from this collection. All of Jessie's earlier letters are also missing.

Jessie's family home, Bertrohill in Shettleston, circa 1910

Bertrohill

Shettleston

12th September

My darling

I want you to have this wee message before you go just to carry with you on the journey tomorrow. Dear, these last days have been perfect ones and the memory of them will be with me always - and with you too won't they laddie? There's good luck for all your journey, dear and any time you are weary just remember that you carry all my love and my thoughts with you. The only thing you have forgotten to take away with you is that dear loving heart of yours but it's in safe keeping isn't it? What a great big strong love there is in our lives, my husband and we'll stick anything so long as we have that, and I know we'll have it always. One thing more - don't forget that I'm your second in command and give me heaps and heaps of things to do.

Till the next time, then, my own laddie! All my heart to you. Ever and ever yours,
Jess

Bertrohill
Shettleston
23rd September 1917

My dearest

Dr May is coming up unofficially this afternoon so I must write your letter before she comes and then she'll post it for me. See! Another good point about doing it just now is that the boy is asleep and I have just got old you to think about. Thanks, darling for that last letter of yours. It was good hearing from you again, dearie, because it is always this first week that's the loneliest. However, we're back to it again and we have to live in our letters till the next time, haven't we? But there's another good memory added to our long, long list. I'm glad it was so happy for you dear, for that is what I wanted it to be - just all happiness - and you are to have a whole long lifetime of it. You made it all so good for me too, boy. I meant to tell you that day when you were going but I had to look as if I didn't care a - and I knew you would understand. Anyway, I tell you now - with the customary rites. You seem to have had rather a busy time all the way back and I'm thinking of you now back into the thick of it.

Don't forget that promise you gave me, and give me heaps and heaps of things to do for you. I'll even knit socks as you suggested altho' I wouldn't guarantee them far. I just want always to be doing something for you and that's how I'm going to spoil you absolutely and literally - come along with the chorus now - My old woman's a --- do you never wish that your wife would write a sensible letter? Oh, do you!

Well, I am once more in command here for Mama went off to Ardeonaig on Friday so I'll be quite busy till she comes back again at the end of November. Winnie is going up beside her for a fortnight till the session opens. The Prelim Latin wasn't so bad and Winnie is quite hopeful about it. Well, dear, must get tea ready now. Coming for some scones?

All my love to you and a kiss from your wee boy. Yours,
Jess

Bertrohill
Shettleston
30th September 1917

My dearest

I had just settled down this afternoon to write to you when there was the usual Sunday afternoon interruption - visitors - and I haven't had a quiet minute till now -

9 o'clock - and your letter won't go tonight. Sorry, dearest. I should have written sooner but on Friday I had to go off to bed. Thought I was in for a chill or something of the kind but I have managed to stave it off and I'm nearly right again. The boy was so startled at seeing Mummy in bed that he has been quite subdued and his angelic mood hasn't worn off yet. I'm afraid tho' that it can't last much longer.

And how are you now, dear one? Quite right again? I hope you won't have any more bother with your teeth for these things are miserably sore. I expect you'll be back again with your company and I know you will be happier. One of these days, old man, I'll be jealous of that company. Hope it knows how lucky it is! Dear, I'm wondering a lot about where you are and what you are doing but I feel sure it's all right with you. I had a letter from your mater on Thursday and I was terribly sorry to hear she had been ill for it will have made these days all the drearier for her.

I wish I could be of some use to her dear. Is there nothing I could do? Wish I could talk to you for a wee while.

I'm sending you one of the snaps, dearie. I sent the other one to your mother for I thought she'd like to have it. You'll have one too as soon as I get some more prints made. Isn't this one good?

All my love and my thoughts to you my darling.

Your Jess

Bertrohill

2nd October 1917

My dearest

One wee letter before I go off to bed! I have had a busy day and I'm a *'ee* bit tired but I must finish off decently by talking to you for a bit. Do you think you'll manage to stick having another old letter so soon again?

I had a note from *Unky* Tim this morning asking me to meet him in town on Friday afternoon. I'm sorry he won't be able to come out to see the boy but better luck next time! We'll have a decent talk anyway. What an age it is since I saw him! Almost a year now. We got news on Monday of Arnold's Captaincy. Yours was in the Gazette that morning too. Funny they should come together like that isn't it? You're all right now laddie! No 'acting' nor *nuffin* about it. It surely hasn't taken so long as you thought it would. Please stop for a minute, dear, and take my special congratulations. You know how they come.

The boy is in good form these days. That last tooth is thro' properly now and he's much happier. We found a Peter Pan book the other day and he has been terribly interested in all the pictures. Papa does Captain Hook for him too, much to his amusement. I have to tell him the *'tory* at all sorts of odd moments thro' the day.

Well, Daddy. I would give a lot just to catch a glimpse of you tonight and see how it is with you. But it's no use wishing as we know, boy.

Here's all of my love to you, and goodnight, my darling. Ever your

Jess

Shettleston

5th October 1917

My darling

I'm just back tonight from town after seeing *Unky* Tim and now that I have tucked the wee laddie into his cot I'll give you all my news. Tim and I had about two hours together this afternoon and I did enjoy seeing him again. It felt too, as if I were getting nearer to you somehow today - talking with Tim about you, dear one. He has promised to come thro' again whenever there's a chance for the special purpose of seeing our wee laddie. *Unky* Tim is terribly interested in him. We had quite a heap of news to exchange and the time passed all too quickly. But I'm looking forward to the next visit.

On my way home I went up to Jarvie's for this morning I had a note from Nancy telling me of a very bad accident her father had last Monday. His right foot was terribly crushed in the hoist and they were afraid at first that he would lose it altogether. However the operation is over and the doctor has managed to save it. He has suffered horribly with it. Nan had just seen him this afternoon and he was better a bit but still feeling the after effects of the chloroform. He is in the Central Nursing Home, Blythswood Sq. but Mrs. J. expects to have him home in about a fortnight or so but it will be long enough before he's right. Isn't it beastly, dear? I know you'll be vexed about it.

Whenever I get more news of him I'll tell you. All my love, dearest. I'll be sending off some books etc. at the weekend so look out for them.

Ever your

Jess

Bertrohill

Shettleston

Sunday 7th

My dearest

Thanks ever so much for your letter yesterday. I was trying not to look for it too much but it was good having it before the weekend because that's always such a *"dreich"* time of waiting. You see we don't get letters on Sunday. I just happened to call at the P. Office on Saturday afternoon and there it was for me. You don't say what sort of time you had when you went up to the battalion. I'm glad tho' that you're having or rather have had such a decent rest. Yes, dear the time is passing but it can't go too quickly for us, can it? I have been thinking about you in this beastly cold wet weather, laddie. It has been miserable here and I expect it's just as bad with you...

Monday. Got stuck here last night, dear, for Nan came out for a wee while and this afternoon I had to go to town.

The latest news of Mr. Jarvie is that he's much about the same - suffering a good deal of pain and it's always worse during the night. The foot is now in splints. There aren't any bones really broken but they are all badly crushed and all the fleshy part of the outside of the foot and part of the heel had to be cut away. So much lime and dirt had gone in that the Dr. was afraid of poisoning but it seems to be fairly clean now. Nan says the shock has told a lot on her father but he's amazingly cheerful. He would be terribly bucked if you have time to write, dearie. If you're scarce of time just send me a wee short one and write to Mr. Jarvie rather.

I sent off a very modest parcel to you this afternoon, dearie - two books and some sweets and cigarettes. If you have read the books just pass them on and I'll try again. I haven't an idea what you have read so my shots may be rather wild. Any special ones you'd like?

The boy is keeping fit and quite as lively - just rather so sometimes. Did you like that photograph dear? Your mother was ever so pleased with the one I sent. Must try if it will enlarge decently for I just love it too. One gets rather attached to photographs these days. Well, there's nothing more to tell just now, dear except perhaps that I do love you. Do you mind?

Yours always.

Jess

Shettleston

12th October 1917

(The date on which Hugh was wounded at Passchendaele)

My dearest

I had a too big a rush to get a letter off to you this afternoon before I went out. I was in at the Home seeing Mr. Jarvie for a little - but here it is now, laddie. Your letter came this morning and it was good to have it - thanks, dearest. I'll be thinking of you all the time but I'm sure everything is going to be right. You should have seen the wee laddie's smile when I gave him your kiss. He sent a great big one straight back to you.

And what am I to say to you, dear, for that other wee bit of paper in your letter? It was tremendously good of you, dear old husband. Ready now till I thank you in our own old way! Got that? I'm glad you like the photo too. I was looking out some for Tim last night for he was very keen to have some. Mr. Jarvie fairly chuckled over that wee one I have of you yourself. He was quite cheerful this afternoon when I was in but he's still suffering a good deal and he hasn't an idea that his foot is so bad. Mrs. Jarvie and I met the doctor just as we were coming away and he says the bone is quite exposed now and he can't let the wounds heal for a week or so yet. I'm afraid Mr. J. will always have a limp and it looks as if it will be a beastly long time before he's anything like better.

I haven't told you, have I, about Winnie's achievement this week? She has got an Andrew and Bethia Stewart Bursary £60. Not bad is it? The Higher Latin is safe too - only seven thro' out of about thirty-five. So she's rather bucked just now.

More news again, dearest. I want to get this away to you. All my love and my thoughts.

Yours,

Jess

Shettleston
18th October 1917

My dearest

I had your letter this morning and it has made things look cheerier a bit for yesterday I didn't know what to think. These War Office wires are such beastly uncommunicative things arn't they? Thanks, darling for the letter. Well, it sounds as if you had a real and true *blighty* one as you wanted and I'm perfectly sure you'll be over soon, laddie. Just ask them as a special favour to run you up to Yorkhill! I am so glad dear that you are decently comfortable for I hate to think of you suffering. Makes me want to bear most of it for you. Wish I could come and write all your letters for you so that you wouldn't need to bother. It's just rotten to be away back here where I can't be of any use to my old man. Tell me about anything you want, dear and I'll send it like a shot. You won't have any idea yet how long you'll be at the base.

The boy and I were to have gone to Ardeonaig on Friday for a week but I have put it off till Monday. I'm not keen about going but mama will be disappointed and it will always pass a wee while for her. The wee holiday will do the boy good too. I'll be back here almost as soon as you know that we're going. All my love to you, my own husband. Shut your eyes a minute and I'll steal out beside you.

Your own wife

Chapter 4

"It is the nights that bring the danger for the fever comes and for the last three nights he has been delirious." (Jessie)

As Hugh's condition deteriorates Jessie leaves her son with her mother in Ardeonaig and crosses the Channel to Le Tréport from where she keeps her parents informed of Hugh's progress. Some days later Jessie is joined by Tim, Hugh's brother.

No. 3 General Hospital

B.E.F.

France

26th October 1917

Dearest own Mama

I know Dada will have given you all the news but I want to write you a little note to yourself today - and to my own wee boy. Well I am very glad I am able to give you good news of Hugh today. Yesterday when I saw him he was very much better. The fever and the sickness have gone and the night before he had quite a good sleep - for about the first time and that made a very great difference. It was a great relief to see him more like himself for the day before - on the Tuesday - he was very ill. The leg seems to have settled into a more comfortable position and the pain is considerably less. The Dr. tells me it is a very bad fracture very near the top but he says the danger is past. Hugh will be here for six or eight weeks and then it will take him practically a year to get better. There are special hospitals at home for cases like this and Hugh says he thinks there is one in Scotland.

I have a pass till the 29th and Hugh wants me to get it extended for a day or two if possible. But I will wire Papa when I'm leaving.

And how is my wee boy? Daddy and I talk of him and we both send all our love to him. I hope he isn't bothering you much Gama. Dada and you and all the others have been so good to me that I don't know how I'll ever make up for it.

It is fine I can give you good news today. There's a great load lifted from my heart for on Tuesday I was very anxious. The Red Cross people make things so easy that I have had very little bother so don't worry at all.

There are two other ladies staying just now and it helps a bit to have their company. Their brother is very seriously wounded practically all over but he is out of danger.

Hugh was telling me about Dan MacGregor of the Post Office so I think they would like to know that he didn't suffer at all. He was killed instantly by a shell. Hugh says he was a very good fellow.

I'll put a note in this afternoon before this letter goes so that you may have the latest news. Hugh sends his love to you and to his own wee Micky and you know that I send all mine to you two dear ones.

Ever yours,

Jessie

No. 3 General Hospital

Le Tréport

France

27th October

Dada, dear

Just a note to tell you more fully how Hugh was this afternoon. When we went up at 2 we found him much easier. His wound was dressed about 11 o'clock and they seem to have fixed the leg in a more comfortable position. The pain was much less and I think that when the effect of the morphia clears off he may get a little natural sleep and that will be the first thing that will make any improvement. Tomorrow morning I am going up to have a short walk with the night Sister and she will tell me exactly how Hugh has been thro' the night so I will leave this open till I have spoken to her.

28th. Hugh had some sleep last night without the aid of morphia and Sister thinks he is a little better this morning. He is still sick a bit but that should soon go. I hope it does. I'll write again tonight, Dada.

There is an exceedingly kind letter from Mr. Gillies by today's mail. I shall write to him today.

Ever yours,

Jessie

Postcard dated 31st October 1917. The card is written and addressed by Jessie to her father but is signed by Hugh. It reads, "You will see No 3 Hospital on the top of the cliffs to the right. Also the funicular railway below."

No. 3 General Hospital
Le Tréport
1st November

My dearest Mama

You will be looking for a letter but I know Dada will have given you all the news as he gets it.

Well things are looking brighter since yesterday Mama. Hugh is much improved and I am almost sure that he is on the right road now.

For the last three days the anxiety has been great because Hugh was steadily losing his strength. He could retain no food whatever and even stimulants made him sick. It was terrible to see him looking so worn and his nerves were badly shaken too.

Fortunately the pain was not so severe. On Monday night his strength was so low that they had to resort to feeding by the bowel and to us it seemed a sort of last hope. But Hugh seems to have taken hold of things again and yesterday he was comparatively comfortable and in good spirits. He has managed to retain a little food - milk and meat jelly. It was such a great relief to see him so easy yesterday, Mama. The Dr. tells me too that the wound is much cleaner.

Tell wee lamb Mann that Daddy sends all his love to him. Mummy will soon be home too to her boy. I have an extension to the 5th November and Tim and I will in all probability travel home together - to London at least. It has been so different since Tim came. Just two days ago Hugh was moved into a little room by himself and it has been so much nicer for us all. Hugh is so much happier that way and we can talk of all sorts of things. The man who was along with him before was very reserved and it was very difficult to talk to him.

I'll put in a short note after we see Hugh this afternoon. Our love to you Mama and to the dear wee boy. Is he learning lots of lessons? Daddy was asking me.

Ever yours,

Jessie

Hugh much about the same. There isn't much improvement but I don't think he is any worse, except that he is fevered a bit. Progress is slow but we can only wait patiently. He has been able to take a little more nourishment and has managed to retain it so that is one good thing Mama. The pain is much less severe too.

Love to all you dear ones.

Jessie

No 3 General Hospital

Le Tréport

Wednesday

My dearest Mama

The days are passing but still I have no decided improvement to tell you of. The great thing is tho' that Hugh is holding on so long and I am sure, Mama, that every day that passes will bring him nearer safety. For the last four days now his general condition has been our great cause for fear but Hugh is fighting well altho' the struggle is proving harder than ever we dreamt it would be.

He is still very weak but he is taking a good deal of nourishment in the form of milk, Berger's food with egg in it, albumen water, jelly, and occasionally a little solid. For a time he had very bad attacks of diarrhoea and the food just went thro' him. The Sister was afraid of a recurrence of the dysentery he had before. But it has pulled up a bit now and surely we'll see some difference in the boy soon. Always he keeps his fine spirit and that should help him such a lot.

It is the nights that bring the danger for the fever comes and for the last three nights he has been delirious. The doctor advised Tim and me to stay in the hospital all night so that we would be within call for things have been just hanging in the balance Mama. But this morning Sister thinks there is a slight improvement. Hugh's Night Sister has been so good to me and she has done everything possible for Hugh. All the sisters are splendid and the doctor - Captain Dickinson - is thoroughly capable. He says the wound is draining steadily and doing as well as can be.

Fortunately the hospital is very empty just now and Hugh can have an extra lot of attention for he needs someone with him all day and all night. He is always at his best when we see him in the afternoon but he changes so quickly that we never know what to expect.

However we have never lost hope, altho' we have been very, very near to it and we are not going to, Mama, and I'm sure things are going right now although we can't see far ahead of us.

I hope our wee Micky is being very, very good and helping you Gama. I miss him a lot but I don't think it will be very long now till I can come home to my boy. Here's a great big hug for him and a kiss from Daddy too. The other afternoon Hugh told me he had been dreaming about Loch Tay and about his wee boy.

I hope I'll be back to help you Gama with all your work. I think we'll be leaving here on Monday but I can't be definite at all. You see how uncertain things are. My dear love to you Mama and to the wee boy.

Ever yours,

Jessie

Telegram 12th November 1917

War Office London OHMS

To: Mrs Mann Bertrohill Shettleston Glasgow

Deeply regret to inform you that Capt H.W. Mann Cameron Highlanders died of wounds 12th November the Army Council express their sympathy

Secy War Office

Telegram 17th November 1917

Buckingham Palace OHMS

To: Mrs Mann Berthrohill Shettleston Glasgow

The King and Queen deeply regret the loss you and the army have sustained by the death of your husband in the Service of his country their Majesty(sic) truly sympathise with you in your sorrow

Keeper of the Privy Purse

Photos from top left-hand corner

Hugh's first resting place

An early 1920's photo of the new Mont Huon Cemetery, Le Tréport, Hugh's final resting place

Hugh's tombstone

Mont Huon Cemetery, Le Tréport 1998

War Memorial, The University of Glasgow Chapel

Hugh's name on the War Memorial at The University of Glasgow Chapel

EPILOGUE

Jessie remained with Hugh until the end. He was buried in a military cemetery close to the hospital. A wooden cross with his name inscribed on it marked his grave which was adorned with mistletoe and an artificial crown and many flowers. In 1922 his remains were moved by the Imperial War Graves Commission to a new cemetery which was built on the site where he died, the military hospitals having been demolished when the war finished. Today, the well-kempt Mont Huon Cemetery, on the wind-swept plateau above the chalk cliffs of Le Tréport, is Hugh's final resting place, his gravestone facing across the English Channel.

In the days following Hugh's death a number of letters were written to Jessie by Ruth Robinson, one of the nurses who tended Hugh in his final days. She had clearly become very close to both Hugh and Jessie and is very concerned for Jessie's well-being. She describes to Jessie the many wreaths and flowers which have been placed on Hugh's grave and writes that of all the patients she has had in ten years of nursing "never have I been more grieved or sadder than I am now about your very dear boy. We all loved him. I told Mr Teare last night, that if he had been my own brother I could not have felt it more..." Most poignant of all perhaps are the letters from members of Jessie's own family, especially her parents. "Our hearts are sore for you my dear in your great grief," writes her father, "but you will have the memory with you always that your dear one did his duty nobly and died a hero's death. But I can't say now all I would. That must be left to the days after you come back to us when everyone will do the utmost to soften your loss."

Jessie was not to return to the Schoolhouse at Ardeonaig. Her father in his letter of 15 November 1917 states that he will go north to Ardeonaig "tomorrow and will bring the dear wee boy down with me on Monday. And he'll be here when you come north dearie. He'll comfort you and I do hope he will always be your shield and comfort. All the time you have been away he has been as good as gold. And everyone's heart has gone out to him and to you in your terrible grief. Mama tells me each one has been kinder than another...Mama will start her packing and within a fortnight she will be down with us. Her successor is appointed and was visiting the Schoolhouse on Monday." The last entry in the school's register for Jessie Hunter Reid, Jessie's mother, is 29 November 1917. It would appear that the decision to leave Ardeonaig and return to Shettleston had been taken before Hugh's death, perhaps in anticipation of his being moved to a hospital in Scotland. It is possible however that the decision to return permanently to Shettleston had been taken during Hugh's last short leave.

Tragedy was to strike Jessie a second time. Her young son, "her comfort and shield", Duncan Cameron Mann, a bright young lad attending the High School of Glasgow, was taken ill suddenly at the end of March 1931. Postcards sent by him from hospital to his grandmother Mann reflect his resilient and lively spirit but he died at the end of May in the Royal Infirmary, Glasgow. He was just sixteen.

Jessie and her son Duncan Cameron (Micky) shortly before his
death in 1931

The Reid family, 1918

Back from left: Howard, Winnie, Hector and Alison Hetherington (née Reid), Arnold. *Seated:* Dine, Scott Hetherington (Hector and Alison's son), Jessie Hunter Reid (Jessie's mother), May (Arnold's wife with baby Margaret), William Reid (Jessie's father) with Duncan Cameron (Micky) (Jessie's son), Jessie. *Front sitting:* Alan

ENDNOTES

1. Alison: Jessie's elder sister
2. K: Kiddie (Jessie)
3. Tilly: Tillicoultry in Clackmannanshire
4. Arnold: Jessie's older brother
5. Tim: Hugh's younger and only brother
6. U.F: United Free Church of Scotland
7. Lyn C Davies: The boyfriend of Jessie's younger sister, Winnie. Lyn enlisted with the Scottish Rifles in 1914. He was killed in 1918.
8. Hector: The boyfriend of Alison, Jessie's elder sister. They were wed in early 1914
9. Howard: Jessie's oldest brother
10. Dada: Jessie's father, William Reid
11. O.K: Old Kirk, ie the established Church of Scotland
12. First anniversary of Hugh's father's death
13. Hugh's uncle
14. Winnie: Jessie's sister, next in age to herself
15. Dine: Jessie's youngest sister
16. Alan: Jessie's younger brother
17. From a letter from the High Steward at Cirencester published in the Regimental History.
18. Micky: Duncan Cameron Mann, the son of Hugh and Jessie

BIBLIOGRAPHY

A J P Taylor, *The First World War - An Illustrated History*, George Rainbird Ltd 1963

J A S Grenville, *The Collins History of the World in the Twentieth Century*, Harper Collins Publishers 1994

John Terrain, *The Road to Passchendaele*, Leo Cooper in Association with Secker & Warburg 1977

Chris McCarthy, *Passchendaele - the Day-by-Day Account*, Arms & Armour Press 1995

Christophe Jupon, *Loos-en-Gohelle dans la tourmente, Août 1914 - Août 1917*, Echos Loossois 1996

Historical Records of The Queen's Own Cameron Highlanders: W Blackwood and Sons Ltd 1931

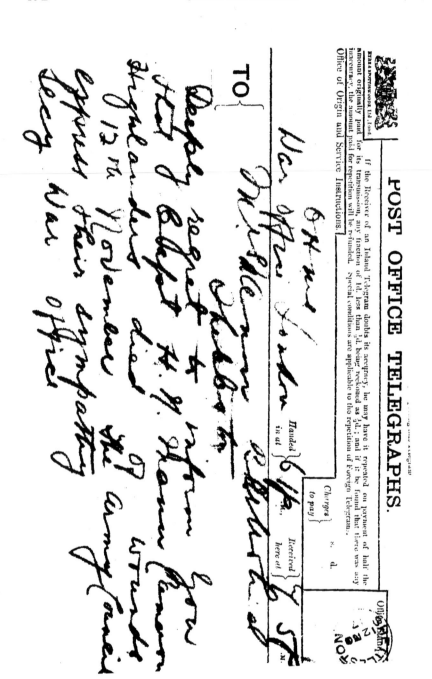